what shall we
cook today?

what shall we cook today?

more than 70 fun and easy
recipes for kids to make

with recipes by

Linda Collister, Liz Franklin, Amanda Grant & Annie Rigg

RYLAND
PETERS
& SMALL

LONDON NEW YORK

Senior Designer Toni Kay
Senior editor Céline Hughes
Picture researcher Emily Westlake
Production Maria Petalidou
Art director Leslie Harrington
Publishing director Alison Starling

First published in the UK in 2011
by Ryland Peters & Small
20–21 Jockey's Fields
London WC1R 4BW
www.rylandpeters.com

10 9 8 7 6 5 4 3 2 1

ISBN: 978-1-84975-102-5

A CIP record for this book is
available from the British Library.

Printed and bound in China

Notes
• All spoon measurements are level, unless
otherwise specified.
• It is generally recommended that free-range
eggs be used. Uncooked or partially cooked
eggs should not be served to the very young,
the very old, those with compromised
immune systems, or to pregnant women.
• Ovens should be preheated to the specified
temperature. Recipes in this book were tested
using a regular oven. If using a fan oven,
follow the manufacturer's instructions for
adjusting temperatures.

contents

introduction

If you've ever woken up wondering how you are going to spend the day and hoping that there are lots of activities on the horizon, get into the kitchen, grab a willing adult and start cooking up a storm!

This book is all about trying new things and learning how to cook great food, with a little help from an adult when you are using an oven, a hob, electrical equipment or anything else that might be tricky or dangerous. You should always ask for help if you are unsure how to do something or you are worried about doing it alone, for example when using a sharp knife. The more help and practice you get, the more confident you will become and soon enough, you'll be making meals for your family with only the minimum of support from Mum or Dad!

Baking cakes, biscuits or scones, putting a curry on the hob to cook, stirring a risotto, whisking egg whites, making filo parcels, rolling out your very own pasta, kneading bread dough and melting chocolate – there's so much fun to be had in the kitchen. Imagine how proud you'll be when you pull your first batch of choc chip cookies from the oven and serve them up at teatime.

A few tips when you're cooking: wear an apron, wash your hands often (especially when handling raw meat), be very careful when using sharp knives, wear thick oven gloves when putting something in or removing from the oven, and keep the work surface clean and tidy. And above all, have fun!

spring

If you are lucky enough to have a vegetable patch or an allotment (or even a big windowsill!), you could try growing your own salad leaves. If not, pick your favourite leaves in the supermarket for this super-easy salad.

green salad with croutons

for the croutons

4 thick slices of brown or
   white bread
2 tablespoons olive oil

for the salad

½ cucumber
about 8 cherry tomatoes
   (of different colours if you
   have them)
4 handfuls of baby spinach
   (or chard) leaves
4 handfuls of rocket leaves
any more of your favourite
   salad leaves

for the dressing

1 tablespoon lemon juice
3 tablespoons olive oil

makes enough for 4

1 To make the croutons, turn the oven on to 180°C (350°F) Gas 4.

2 Cut the slices of bread into small cubes. Put the cubes into a roasting tin, sprinkle the oil over the top and use your hands to mix the bread around in the oil. **Ask an adult to help you** put the tin in the oven and bake for 10 minutes.

3 **Ask an adult to help you** take the tin out of the oven and mix the croutons with a wooden spoon. Put back into the oven for 10 minutes or until the croutons are golden and crunchy.

4 Meanwhile, to make the salad, slice the cucumber into thin slices and cut the tomatoes in half.

5 Wash the spinach (or chard) and rocket and shake gently to get rid of a bit of the water. Put into a big salad bowl with the cucumber and tomatoes and any other salad leaves you'd like to add.

6 In a glass jar or small jug mix together the lemon juice and olive oil for the dressing and drizzle over the salad. Toss everything together with salad serving spoons.

7 Finally, drop in the lovely crispy croutons (add them at the last minute so they don't go soggy in the dressing!) and toss the salad again. Serve immediately.

Sometimes it's a great idea to use very few ingredients in a dish, so that you can really taste and enjoy each ingredient. This is a good example because the sweet cherry tomatoes and fresh basil get a chance to shine. You'll also soon discover that there are some flavours which work so well together that you can always rely on them to make a yummy combination – tomato and basil are definitely a magical pair!

penne with tomatoes, garlic & basil

400 g ripe cherry tomatoes
2 garlic cloves
100 ml olive oil
a small handful of fresh basil
    leaves, torn
400 g dried penne pasta
sea salt and freshly ground
    black pepper

serves 4

1 Cut the tomatoes in half.

2 Peel the garlic cloves and crush them with a garlic crusher.

3 Pop the tomatoes and garlic into a large bowl. Pour over the olive oil. Season with salt and black pepper, add half the basil and leave for an hour or so to infuse. A warmish place is best, or at room temperature, but not the fridge because the cold will stop the oil from absorbing all the lovely flavours.

4 **Ask an adult to help you** cook the pasta. Bring a big saucepan of water to the boil and add a pinch of salt. Drop in the pasta and cook according to the instructions on the packet. The cooked pasta should be 'al dente'.

5 Drain the pasta and add it to the bowl with the infused oil. Toss well so that the oil coats all the pieces and finally stir in the remaining torn basil.

tomato pesto rolls

500 g self-raising flour

½ teaspoon salt

250 g natural cottage cheese

a small handful of fresh basil
leaves, but save 10 leaves
for decoration

1 large egg

about 150 ml milk

5 cherry tomatoes

2 tablespoons Home-made
Pesto (page 130), shop-
bought pesto or olive oil

a baking tray, lined with
baking parchment

makes 10 small rolls

1 Turn the oven on to 190°C (375°F) Gas 5. Sprinkle a little flour over the baking tray and put it to one side.

2 Put the flour, salt, cottage cheese and basil into the bowl of a food processor. **Ask an adult to help you** run the machine until everything is just mixed and looks like crumbs.

3 Break the egg into a jug, pick out any pieces of shell, then add 150 ml milk and beat with a fork, just to combine the egg and milk.

4 **Ask an adult to help you** run the machine and pour in the egg/milk mix through the feed tube. Stop the processor when the ingredients have come together to make a ball of soft dough. If there are dry crumbs and the dough feels hard and dry add a little more milk.

5 Sprinkle a little flour over the work surface. **Ask an adult to help you** remove the processor blade then turn out the dough onto the work surface. Flour your hands, then gently knead the dough twice so it looks smoother.

6 Divide the dough into 10 equal pieces and roll each into a ball. Arrange the balls slightly apart on the prepared baking tray. Make a deep hole in the centre with your finger.

7 Cut the tomatoes in half. Push a basil leaf into each hole, then a tomato half – cut-side up. Make sure the tomato is deep in the hole in the dough (or it will pop right out during baking!). Brush the top of each roll with the pesto or olive oil.

8 **Ask an adult to help you** put the rolls in the oven and bake for about 20 minutes, until they are golden brown.

9 **Ask an adult to help you** take the rolls out of the oven and put them on a wire rack. Leave to cool until just warm. Eat warm, or split in half and toast the next day.

To make sweet fruit rolls: Follow the recipe opposite but leave out the basil, tomatoes and pesto or oil. Instead, add 1 tablespoon of runny honey to the processor with the cottage cheese mixture. Make the dough as in the method opposite, then turn it out onto the work surface. Scatter 3 tablespoons of fresh blueberries, 2 tablespoons of dried cherries or chopped, ready-to-eat dried apricots over the dough and knead them into it. Shape into 10 rolls and arrange on the baking tray then **ask an adult to help you** put them in the oven and bake for about 20 minutes.

The dough for these cute little bread rolls is mixed in a food processor for speed, but you can also make it with your hands. You can either make the rolls savoury (with pesto and tomatoes), and eat them with soup or on their own, or you can make them sweet (with honey, and fresh and dried fruit), to eat as an afternoon treat.

Many breads you make at home need time to rise so that they become light and airy when they are baked, but people in Ireland make soda bread, which needs no kneading or rising. Mixing the flour with acidic buttermilk, which reacts with alkaline bicarbonate of soda, creates bubbles of carbon dioxide.

irish soda bread

450 g good-quality plain
    white flour

1 teaspoon salt

1¼ teaspoons bicarbonate
    of soda

about 350 ml buttermilk
    (or 175 ml each natural
    yoghurt and milk)

a baking tray, lined with
    baking parchment

makes 1 medium loaf

1 Turn the oven on to 220°C (425°F) Gas 7. Sprinkle a little flour over the baking tray and put it to one side.

2 Set a large sieve over a large mixing bowl. Tip the flour into the sieve, add the salt and bicarbonate of soda and sift into the bowl. Make a well in the centre.

3 Pour the buttermilk into the well. Mix everything together with a round-bladed table knife, or with your hands, to make a soft and slightly sticky dough. Don't worry if it looks a bit rough.

4 Sprinkle a little flour over the work surface, then turn out the dough onto it. Flour your hands and gently shape the dough into a ball.

5 Put the ball of dough on the prepared baking tray and flatten it so it is about 3–4 cm high. Using the same table knife, score a big cross on top of the loaf – this will make it easier to tear it into quarters when it is baked.

6 **Ask an adult to help you** put the loaf in the oven and bake for about 35 minutes, until a good golden brown. **Ask an adult to help you** remove it from the oven and tip it upside

down onto a wire rack, then tap the underside with your knuckles. The loaf is cooked if it sounds hollow. If it sounds like a dull 'thud', bake it for 5 minutes more. Leave to cool on the wire rack until cool enough to slice.

To make speckled white soda bread: Add 100 g chopped dark chocolate or chocolate chips, and 1 tablespoon caster sugar to the bowl with the sifted flour. Mix, then finish the recipe as above.

To make brown soda bread: The coarse brown wheaten flour traditionally used is hard to find outside Ireland, but a mix of plain wholemeal flour (stoneground if possible), white flour and wheatbran and wheatgerm (from wholefood shops) works well. To make a brown loaf, replace the white flour in the recipe for white soda bread (see left) with 200 g good-quality plain white flour, 200 g plain wholemeal flour and 50 g wheatbran and wheatgerm mix or 25 g of each. Follow the recipe by mixing all the dry ingredients together (but don't sift them into the bowl), then mix to a soft dough with the buttermilk. Shape and bake the loaf as for the white soda bread loaf.

Italian crostini

4 large thick slices of bread

12 cherry tomatoes or baby
plum tomatoes

4 fresh basil leaves

8 pitted black olives

3 tablespoons olive oil

1 large garlic clove

freshly ground black pepper

a large baking tray

makes 4

1 Turn the oven on to its hottest setting, usually 240°C (475°F) Gas 9. Arrange the slices of bread on the baking tray.

2 **Ask an adult to help you** put the bread in the oven and bake for 5 minutes, until golden brown. **Ask an adult to help you** remove the tray from the oven and put the bread slices onto serving plates.

3 Cut the tomatoes into quarters. Put into a small mixing bowl. Tear up the basil leaves into little pieces and add to the tomatoes. Quarter the olives and add to the bowl with the olive oil and black pepper. Stir gently to mix.

4 Slice the garlic clove in half and rub the cut sides over the hot bread, making sure the bread isn't too hot to hold. Spoon the tomato mixture over the bread and eat straightaway.

Some more ideas

Drain a 200-g tin of tuna and flake the fish with a fork. Arrange the fish on top of the tomato mixture.

Cut a 150-g ball of mozzarella cheese into small cubes. Arrange the cubes on top of the tomato mixture.

Top the tomato mixture with rocket leaves and 100 g thinly sliced ham.

Drain a 200-g tin of tuna and **ask an adult to help you** put it in the bowl of a food processor with 2 anchovy fillets, the juice of a lemon, 2 tablespoons mayonnaise and several grinds of black pepper. Process to make a thick paste and spread over the bread.

Crostini are Italian snacks, similar to sandwiches, but you take a slice of toasted bread and put yummy things on top. You never put another slice of bread on top, so you have to be careful when you are eating it that the topping doesn't fall off! It's tastier if you use nice, crusty bread that is a day old.

This is an ideal recipe to get you into filo pastry, which is great for filling. It's a ready-made pastry which looks like sheets of paper and becomes crisp and crumbly when it's baked. It's easy to use and you don't have to mix it or roll it out – just don't uncover it until the last moment or it will get very dry.

salmon filo parcels

4 pieces of skinless salmon
fillet, about 125 g each

40 g unsalted butter, at room
temperature

2 small pieces or 1 large piece
of stem ginger in syrup,
about 25 g

200 g filo pastry, thawed
if necessary

sea salt and freshly ground
black pepper

1 lemon, to serve

a large ovenproof baking dish,
lightly greased

makes 4

1 Turn the oven on to 190°C (375°F) Gas 5.

2 Rinse the 4 pieces of salmon under the cold tap, then pat dry with kitchen paper.

3 Put the butter in a small bowl and stir with a teaspoon until soft. Lift the ginger out of the syrup and put it on a small plate. Using a small knife, cut the ginger into thin slices, then cut the slices into strips. Add the ginger to the butter, then add some salt and pepper and mix well. Divide the mixture into 4 equal pieces.

4 Unwrap the filo pastry and separate and count the sheets. You will need an equal number for each parcel. Brands of filo vary from shop to shop, and each brand has different sized sheets, but arrange the sheets to make 4 rectangles, about 30 x 25 cm by overlapping or folding the sheets. If you have to cut sheets in half, use kitchen scissors.

5 Put a piece of fish right in the middle of each rectangle. Spread a portion of the butter on top of each piece of fish. Fold the pastry over the fish as if you were wrapping up a Christmas parcel, then fold the ends underneath. Arrange the parcels in the prepared dish.

6 **Ask an adult to help you** put the dish in the oven and bake for 25 minutes, or until golden brown. **Ask an adult to help you** take the dish out of the oven.

7 Serve the parcels hot on 4 plates, together with the lemon cut into 4 wedges.

Whether you make this soup with fresh or frozen peas, it's quick as well as delicious!

creamy pea soup

1 small onion
1 small potato (about 100 g)
1 garlic clove
3 tablespoons olive oil
700 g peas (fresh or frozen)
1 litre well-flavoured
   vegetable or chicken stock
3 tablespoons double cream
sea salt and freshly ground
   black pepper
3 tablespoons olive oil,
   to drizzle
crusty bread, to serve

serves 4

1 Peel the onion and chop it into fairly small pieces. Peel the potato and chop it into small, even-sized pieces. Peel the garlic clove and crush it with a garlic crusher.

2 **Ask an adult to help you** heat the olive oil in a large saucepan, then add the onion, garlic and potato. Cook over gentle heat for about 8–10 minutes, stirring quite often, until the onion is shiny and the potatoes are starting to soften.

3 Pour in the peas and the stock.

4 Leave the soup to simmer for about 20 minutes, until the potato is very soft – the potatoes should easily be squashed when you press them with a wooden spoon.

5 **Ask an adult to help you** remove the saucepan from the heat and liquidize the soup with a stick blender until it is smooth.

6 If you don't have a stick blender and are using a food processor or blender, you must let the soup cool a little before you blend it. Very hot soup can expand in the machine and may cause a nasty burn if you fill the machine too full.

7 Once the soup is nice and smooth, stir in the cream and season with a little salt and black pepper.

8 Spoon the mixture into pretty mugs or soup bowls, garnish with a drizzle of olive oil and serve with some good crusty bread.

pea, sausage & onion wraps

250 g good-quality sausages

1 onion

2 garlic cloves

2 ripe tomatoes

6 tablespoons olive oil

150 g peas (fresh, or frozen
and defrosted)

4 small flour tortillas

3 tablespoons mascarpone

1 small egg

sea salt and freshly ground
black pepper

a pastry brush

serves 4

1 **Ask an adult to help you** cut away the skins of the sausages with kitchen scissors and throw the skins away. Pull the sausagemeat into chunks, put in a bowl and set aside.

2 Peel the onion and chop it finely. Peel the garlic cloves and crush them with a garlic crusher. Slice the top off the tomatoes and squeeze out the seeds. Chop the flesh into small pieces.

3 **Ask an adult to help you** heat half of the olive oil in a saucepan and fry the onion and garlic over gentle heat for 3–4 minutes, until the onion is starting to soften.

4 Add the sausagemeat and season with salt and black pepper. Cook for 1–2 minutes longer, until the sausagemeat is golden. Give it all a good stir every once in a while.

5 Add the tomatoes and peas to the pan. Stir well and cook for another 15 minutes or so,

until all the liquid has disappeared, the meat is cooked and the mixture is deliciously sticky.

6 Lay the tortillas out on a chopping board and spoon one-quarter of the mixture onto one side of each tortilla, leaving a 2-cm border around the edges. Dot little bits of mascarpone over the sausagemeat mixture.

7 Break the egg into a bowl, pick out any pieces of shell, then beat lightly with a fork until smooth.

8 Brush some beaten egg around the edge of the tortillas with a pastry brush. Fold over each tortilla to make a semi-circle shape. Press the edges down to seal them.

9 **Ask an adult to help you** heat the remaining oil in a large frying pan over medium heat and fry the tortillas for 3–4 minutes on each side, until golden. Drain on kitchen paper before eating.

These wraps make
a nice change from
sandwiches and
they're filling
enough for dinner.
Eat them warm
from the pan and
wrapped in a napkin
to prevent the filling
from escaping!

A frittata is an Italian omelette, usually made in a large frying pan, but these little ones are more fun because these are baked in a muffin tin – perfect if you are having friends round.

mini vegetable frittatas

4 spring onions

3 medium courgettes

1 medium red pepper

100 g soft sun-dried tomatoes

125 g Fontina cheese (or
　Gruyère or Swiss cheese)

8 large eggs

125 ml single cream

2 tablespoons olive oil

a good pinch of dried oregano

freshly ground black pepper

a 12-hole muffin tin, well
　greased or 12 flexible
　muffin moulds

a baking tray

makes 12

1　Turn the oven on to 180°C (350°F) Gas 4.

2　Carefully trim the hairy root ends off the spring onions, and the dark green leafy tops. Rinse the onions well under the cold tap, and drain thoroughly. Slice into thin rounds, then put to one side.

3　Rinse the courgettes, then trim off the ends. Slice each courgette in half lengthways then cut each half in half lengthways so you have 4 long strips from each courgette. Cut the strips across to make 1-cm pieces. Put with the spring onions.

4　Rinse the red pepper. Cut off the stalk end, then cut the pepper in half and pull out the core with its seeds. Slice the red flesh of the pepper into strips about 1 cm wide, then cut each strip across to make 1-cm pieces. Add to the onions.

5　Cut the sun-dried tomatoes into 1-cm pieces but keep separate from the onion mixture.

6　Cut the cheese into 1-cm cubes and add to the tomatoes.

7　Break the eggs into a bowl, pick out any pieces of shell, then pour the cream in. Add several grinds of black pepper then, using a table fork, gently beat the eggs and cream together until thoroughly mixed.

8　**Ask an adult to help you** heat the olive oil in a frying pan over low heat. Fry the spring onions, courgettes, red pepper and a good pinch of oregano and stir well with a wooden spoon. Turn up the heat to medium and cook for 5 minutes, stirring carefully every minute, until the vegetables are a light golden brown. **Ask an adult to help you** remove the pan from the heat.

9　Leave to cool for 5 minutes then stir in the tomatoes and cheese.

10　Set the muffin tin on a baking tray. Spoon the vegetable and cheese mixture into the holes, filling each one with an equal amount. Using a small ladle or spoon, pour the egg mix over the vegetable mixture (you may find it easier to transfer the egg mix to a large jug then pour the mix onto the vegetables).

11　**Ask an adult to help you** put the frittatas in the oven and bake for 25 minutes, until puffed, golden and set.

12　**Ask an adult to help you** remove the tin from the oven. Leave to cool for 5 minutes, then gently run a round-bladed knife around the inside of each muffin hole. Carefully lift out or tip out onto a serving platter. Serve warm or at room temperature.

Koftas are like meatballs, but they come from regions like the Middle East, South Asia and North Africa. They differ from meatballs in that they are made with some of the spices that originate in those regions, and they are usually cooked on skewers. Eat them with pita bread and yoghurt dip.

lamb koftas with pita pockets

500 g lean minced lamb

1 small red onion

2 teaspoons mild paprika

1½ teaspoons ground coriander

1½ teaspoons ground cumin

¼ teaspoon ground cinnamon

a few sprigs of fresh flat leaf parsley or coriander

sea salt and freshly ground black pepper

for the dip

200 ml natural yoghurt

a small handful of fresh chives

a few sprigs of fresh flat leaf parsley or coriander

8 small or picnic-sized pitas, to serve

16 wooden skewers

a baking tray or roasting tin, lined with foil and oiled

serves 4

1 Turn the oven on to 220°C (425°F) Gas 7. Soak the skewers in a bowl of water (this stops the wood from burning in the oven). Meanwhile, make up the meat mix.

2 Tip the minced lamb into a large mixing bowl. Peel the skin away from the onion and throw it away. Carefully grate the onion onto the lamb using the large holes of a grater.

3 Measure the spices – paprika, ground coriander, ground cumin, ground cinnamon – and some black pepper and salt into the bowl. Using kitchen scissors, snip the parsley or coriander sprigs into the bowl. Put your hands into the bowl and mix together all the ingredients, squeezing it between your fingers until it looks evenly mixed. (If you have plenty of time you can now cover the bowl and chill it in the fridge for up to 5 hours before finishing the recipe.)

4 Divide the meat mixture into 16 even portions. Using your hands, mould each portion of meat around a skewer to make an egg or sausage shape about 10 cm long. Arrange the skewers on the prepared baking tray. Wash your hands thoroughly.

5 **Ask an adult to help you** put the baking tray in preheated oven and bake for about 15 minutes, or until well browned.

6 While the meat is cooking, make the dip by mixing the yoghurt with some salt and pepper. Snip the chives and parsley or coriander into small pieces with kitchen scissors and mix into the yoghurt. Spoon into a serving bowl.

7 When the koftas are ready, **ask an adult to help you** lift the tray out of the oven. Transfer the skewers to a serving plate and serve with the yoghurt dip and warm pitas.

Serve these tasty chicken (or turkey) meatballs with the Thai fragrant rice opposite and a little bowl of sweet chilli sauce, which is a bit like Thai tomato ketchup, for dipping.

thai meatballs with chicken

50 g fresh bread (about
    2 medium slices)
500 g minced chicken
    or turkey
1 egg
2 spring onions
½ teaspoon ground coriander
a small handful of fresh
    coriander leaves
1 teaspoon fish sauce or
    soy sauce
2 teaspoons sweet chilli
    sauce, plus extra for
    serving
a large baking dish, oiled

makes 12

1 Turn the oven on to 200°C (400°F) Gas 6.

2 Tear up the bread and put it into a blender or processor. **Ask an adult to help you** run the machine until the bread turns into crumbs. Tip the crumbs into a bowl. Add the minced chicken or turkey. Break the egg into the bowl and pick out any pieces of shell.

3 Carefully trim the hairy root ends off the spring onions, and the dark green leafy tops. Rinse the onions well under the cold tap, and drain thoroughly. Slice into thin rounds. Add to the bowl, then add the ground coriander.

4 Using kitchen scissors, snip the fresh coriander leaves straight into the bowl.

Add the fish sauce or soy sauce and the sweet chilli sauce to the bowl. Mix well with your hands then roll the mixture into small balls – use about 1 tablespoon of mixture for each.

5 Arrange the meatballs in the oiled baking dish. **Ask an adult to help you** put it into the oven and bake for 25 minutes until golden brown and cooked all the way through.

6 While the meatballs are cooking, wash your hands well, then make the rice (opposite).

7 Serve the meatballs straight from the baking dish with the rice and extra sweet chilli sauce in a little bowl for dipping.

thai fragrant rice

250 g Thai fragrant rice
a pinch of salt

enough for 4

1 **Ask an adult to help** with this recipe because it involves boiling water.

2 Fill a large saucepan half full with water and put it on the hob. Cover with a lid, then turn on the heat and leave until the water boils (about 5 to 10 minutes).

3 Carefully pour the rice into the water, add the salt and stir gently. When the water starts to boil again, turn the heat down so the water doesn't bubble over the sides of the pan.

4 Leave to boil gently (this is called simmering) for 10 minutes. Alternatively, follow the directions on the packet.

5 Make sure the sink is empty, then set a colander in the middle. **Ask an adult** to pour the saucepan rice into the colander. Shake the colander well to drain off all the water, then tip the rice into a serving bowl and serve straightaway with the Thai meatballs.

You might like to make these buns one weekend for everyone to enjoy as an afternoon treat, or for a late, lazy breakfast on Sunday. They are rolled up with sugar, cinnamon and pecans or raisins then cut into spiral buns. Warm from the oven, they smell and taste heavenly. The dough can be made with your hands or using a large electric mixer fitted with a special 'dough hook'.

sticky cinnamon buns

for the dough

500 g strong white bread
   flour

1 x 7-g sachet easy-blend
   (fast-action) dried yeast

1 teaspoon salt

3 tablespoons caster sugar

1 large egg, at room
   temperature

300 ml milk, lukewarm

40 g unsalted butter,
   very soft

for the filling

30 g unsalted butter,
   very soft

1 teaspoon ground cinnamon

4 tablespoons light
   muscovado sugar

50 g pecan pieces or raisins

a baking tray, very well
   greased

makes 12 buns

1 For the dough, put the flour in a large mixing bowl. Add the yeast, salt and sugar and mix everything with your hands or **ask an adult to help you** with the electric mixer dough hook. Make a well in the centre.

2 Mix the egg with the milk and add to the bowl with the very soft butter.

3 Using your hand, slowly stir the flour into the liquid in the hollow, then work the mixture with your hand until all the flour has been mixed in. Flours vary so if there are dry crumbs in the bowl and the dough feels dry add a little more milk, a tablespoonful at a time. If the dough is very sticky add a little more flour. If using the electric mixer use the lowest speed.

4 When the mixture comes together to make a soft dough, gather it into a ball. Sprinkle a little flour over the work surface, then turn out the dough onto it. Flour your hands and gently knead the dough, stretching it out then gathering back into a ball, for 5 minutes. The dough can be kneaded using an electric mixer on low speed for 4 minutes.

5 Put the dough back into the mixing bowl and cover the bowl with a snap-on lid or put the bowl into a large, clean plastic bag and tie it closed. Leave the bowl near a warm hob or above a radiator until doubled in size – about 1 hour. It will take longer at normal room temperature or on a cool day.

6 Uncover the bowl and gently punch down the dough with your fist. Sprinkle a little flour over the work surface, then turn out the dough onto it.

7 Using your hands, or a rolling pin, press or roll the dough out to a rectangle about 25 x 35 cm. Spread the butter for the filling over the dough. Mix the cinnamon and sugar together, then sprinkle over the butter. Lastly, scatter the nuts or raisins over the dough and lightly press down.

8 Roll up the dough from one of the long sides (like a Swiss roll) to make a long roll, then pinch the 'seam' of the dough to seal it. **Ask an adult to help you** cut it into 12 equal pieces.

9 Put the rolls slightly apart on the prepared baking tray with the cut side facing up so you can see the spiral filling. Cover the tray with a clean, dry tea towel and leave to rise for 20 minutes. Meanwhile, turn the oven on to 220°C (425°F) Gas 7.

10 Uncover the buns, then **ask an adult to help you** put the tray in the oven and bake for 20 minutes, until golden brown. **Ask an adult to help you** remove the tray from the oven. Use a metal spatula to lift the buns onto a wire rack to cool. Eat warm or at room temperature. Once they are cold you can keep the buns in an airtight container and eat them within 2 days or freeze them for up to 1 month.

This is a clever cake, because it makes great use of a whole orange: half of it is whizzed in a food processor and put in the cake mix to make it extra orangey; the other half is used for a topping. Wash it well before using.

fresh orange cake

1 unwaxed or organic orange, washed

175 g unsalted butter, very soft

250 g caster sugar

3 large eggs, at room temperature

250 g self-raising flour

1 teaspoon bicarbonate of soda

100 ml milk

3 tablespoons natural yoghurt (full-fat or low-fat, but not fat-free)

3 tablespoons caster or granulated sugar, for the topping

a 900-g loaf tin, greased greaseproof paper or non-stick baking parchment

makes 1 large loaf cake

1 Turn the oven on to 180°C (350°F) Gas 4. Cut a long strip of greaseproof paper or non-stick baking parchment the width of the greased loaf tin. Press the paper into the tin so it covers the base and the two short sides.

2 Carefully cut the orange in half. Save one half for the topping. Remove the pips from the other half, then cut it into 8 pieces. Put the pieces, as they are with the skin still on, in a food processor and **ask an adult to help you** run the machine until the orange is chopped into very small pieces. **Ask an adult to help you** remove the blade from the processor, then transfer the orange mixture to a mixing bowl or the bowl of an electric mixer.

3 Add the very soft butter and sugar to the bowl. Break the eggs into a small bowl, pick out any pieces of shell, then pour the eggs into the mixing bowl.

4 Set a sieve over the bowl. Spoon the flour and bicarbonate of soda into the sieve, then sift into the bowl. Add the milk and yoghurt then beat with a wooden spoon or electric mixer (on low speed) for 1 minute until well mixed and there are no streaks of flour visible.

5 Spoon the mixture into the prepared loaf tin and spread the surface to make it smooth.

6 **Ask an adult to help you** put the cake in the oven and bake for about 50 minutes, until a good golden brown. To test if the cake is cooked, **ask an adult to help you** remove it from the oven, then push a cocktail stick into the centre. If the stick comes out clean, then the cake is ready. If it is sticky with mixture, then cook the cake for another 5 minutes.

7 While the cake is baking, make the topping. Squeeze out the juice from the reserved orange half with a lemon squeezer. Pour the juice into a small bowl, add the sugar and stir for a minute to make a thick, syrupy glaze.

8 When the cake is cooked, **ask an adult to help you** remove it from the oven and stand the tin on a wire rack. Prick the top of the cake all over with a cocktail stick to make lots of small holes in it. Spoon the orange syrup all over the top so it trickles into the holes. Leave until completely cold before carefully removing the cake from the tin. Peel off the lining paper. Cut the cake into thick slices. Store your cake in an airtight container and eat it within 4 days.

chocolate fudge birthday cake

for the cake

250 g plain flour

2 teaspoons baking powder

1 teaspoon bicarbonate
   of soda

a pinch of salt

100 g good dark chocolate

3 tablespoons cocoa powder

100 ml water, very hot but
   not boiling

175 g unsalted butter,
   softened

250 g caster sugar

3 large eggs

200 ml natural yoghurt
   (full-fat or low-fat, but
   not fat-free)

your choice of edible
   decorations

for the chocolate icing

100 ml double cream

50 g good milk chocolate

50 g good dark chocolate

a springform cake tin,
   22.5 cm diameter, greased
   greaseproof paper or non-
   stick baking parchment

makes 8–10 slices

1 Turn the oven on to 160°C (325°F) Gas 3. Put the greased cake tin on a sheet of greaseproof paper or non-stick baking parchment and draw around it. Using scissors, cut inside the line so you have a circle the same size as the tin. Fit this into the bottom of the tin.

2 Set a large sieve over a bowl and tip the flour, baking powder, bicarbonate of soda and salt into the sieve. Carefully sift these ingredients into the bowl. Set the bowl aside.

3 Break up the dark chocolate and put it into a large heatproof mixing bowl. Mix in the cocoa powder. **Ask an adult to help you** pour on the very hot water. Leave for 1 minute then stir gently with a wooden spoon until the mixture is very smooth and melted. Put on one side.

4 Put the butter and sugar into the bowl of an electric mixer (in which case you will need **an adult to help**) or a mixing bowl. Beat well with the whisk attachment or a wooden spoon.

5 Break the eggs into a small bowl, remove any pieces of shell, then gradually add to the bowl and beat really well until very smooth.

6 Pour the melted chocolate mixture into the bowl and mix well. Spoon in the yoghurt and tip in the flour mixture and mix well.

7 Spoon the mixture into the prepared tin, then spread the mixture evenly so it is smooth.

8 **Ask an adult to help you** put the cake in the oven and bake for 55 minutes. To test if the cake is cooked, **ask an adult to help you** remove it from the oven, then push a cocktail stick into the centre. If the stick comes out clean, then the cake is ready. If it is sticky with mixture, then cook the cake for another 5 minutes.

9 **Ask an adult to help you** remove the cake from the oven and set the tin on a wire rack. Leave to cool for 5 minutes then loosen the cake by running a round-bladed knife inside the tin. Unclip the tin and leave the cake to cool completely. Don't worry if it sinks a bit.

10 To make the chocolate icing, put the cream into a saucepan. **Ask an adult to help you** heat it until it is scalding hot, but not quite boiling. Remove the pan from the heat. Break up the two kinds of chocolate and put it in a heatproof bowl. Carefully pour over the hot cream. Leave for about 2 minutes, then stir until smooth. Leave to cool – the icing will thicken as it cools.

11 Set the cake upside down on a serving plate. Spread the icing on the top and sides of the cake to cover completely. Cover with your choice of edible decorations. Leave in a cool place until it is firm before you cut it. Store in an airtight container and eat it within 5 days.

Get ahead and make this brilliantly chocolatey birthday cake the day before the party. Decorate it any way you like, but don't forget the candles!

These chewy, tasty cookies are made with the same oats that you eat at breakfast time. Why not make a box of these cookies for a friend to take round to their house? You can add raisins, dried cherries and cranberries, chopped nuts or chocolate chips.

oatie cookies

125 g unsalted butter

100 g caster sugar

100 g dark muscovado sugar

1 large egg

150 g porridge oats

125 g plain flour

a pinch of salt

¼ teaspoon bicarbonate of soda

½ teaspoon vanilla extract

75 g raisins, dried cherries, dried cranberries, chopped nuts or chocolate chips

2 non-stick baking trays, greased

makes 18 cookies

1 Turn the oven on to 180°C (350°F) Gas 4.

2 Put the butter in a saucepan that's big enough to hold all the ingredients. **Ask an adult to help you** melt the butter over low heat. Remove the pan from the heat and put it on a heatproof work surface. Tip both the sugars into the pan and mix into the butter with a wooden spoon. Make sure you stir until all the lumps of sugar have been broken up.

3 Break the egg into a bowl, pick out any pieces of shell, then beat lightly with a fork until smooth. Pour the egg into the pan and mix it in.

4 Add the porridge oats to the pan and stir well. Add the flour, salt, bicarbonate of soda and vanilla extract and mix well.

5 Finally, add your choice of dried fruit, nuts or chocolate and mix until thoroughly combined.

6 Using a rounded tablespoon of mixture for each cookie, drop the mixture onto the prepared baking trays, making sure they are spaced well apart because they will spread when they bake. Gently flatten the mounds of dough with your fingers. **Ask an adult to help you** put the cookies in the oven and bake for 13–15 minutes, until lightly browned.

7 **Ask an adult to help you** remove the trays from the oven. Leave to cool for about 2 minutes, then use a metal spatula to lift the cookies off the trays and onto a wire rack to cool completely. Store your cookies in an airtight container and eat them within 5 days.

These pancake parcels are filled with sticky pears and mascarpone, a thick Italian cream.

baked pancake parcels with pears & mascarpone

30 g unsalted butter

for the pancakes
30 g unsalted butter
2 medium eggs
300 ml milk
a pinch of salt
120 g plain flour, sifted

for the filling
500 g mascarpone
3 ripe but firm pears
4 tablespoons dark runny
   honey (chestnut, if
   possible)

an ovenproof dish, greased

serves 4

1 To make the pancakes, **ask an adult to help you** melt the butter in a pan, then pour it into the bowl of a food processor or in a blender with the eggs and milk and run the machine to combine.

2 Sift the salt and flour into the machine and whiz until you have a smooth batter. Set aside for 30 minutes–1 hour.

3 **Ask an adult to help you** cook the pancakes. Put a little of the butter for frying in a small non-stick frying pan and heat over medium heat until hot. If the batter has thickened, you may need to add a little water.

4 Pour in a small amount of batter (just enough to cover the base of the pan) and tilt the pan to spread the mixture evenly. Cook for 1–2 minutes, until the pancake is golden on the underside and little bubbles have started to appear on the surface. Using a spatula, loosen the pancake around the edges and turn it over. Cook for another minute, until golden brown.

5 Repeat until all the remaining batter has been used up – it should make 8 pancakes. Keep adding butter a little at a time between pancakes to keep the frying pan greased.

6 Put the finished pancakes on top of a large sheet of aluminium foil and stack them between layers of greaseproof paper. Wrap up the foil and put the parcel in a low oven until you are ready to use the pancakes.

7 To make the filling, put the mascarpone in a large bowl and beat until smooth, then remove 3 tablespoons to another small bowl.

8 Peel the pears, cut them into quarters and then cut away the cores. Chop the flesh into small pieces. Fold them lightly into the large bowl of mascarpone. Fold in 2 tablespoons of the honey very lightly to give a rippled effect.

9 Turn the grill on and wait for it to heat up. Remove the pancakes from the oven and lay one out flat on a chopping board. Spoon an eighth of the pear mixture onto the centre. Fold into a flat parcel and put in the greased ovenproof dish, seam-side down. Repeat with the remaining pancakes.

10 Dot the remaining mascarpone over the parcels and drizzle over the last of the honey. **Ask an adult to help you** put the dish under the hot grill and leave for 4 minutes, or until golden and bubbling.

You'll think summer has arrived early when you make these little icy treats! It helps if you have an ice-cream maker, but you can still easily make them without one.

little lemon iced yoghurt sandwiches

50 g dark chocolate

for the iced yoghurt

1 large, juicy unwaxed or
    organic lemon, washed

500 ml natural yoghurt
    (full-fat)

100 g caster sugar

for the wafers

50 g unsalted butter, softened

50 g caster sugar

2 egg whites

50 g plain flour

an ice-cream maker (optional)

2 baking trays, lined with
    baking parchment

makes about 6

1 To make the iced yoghurt, carefully grate the zest into a large bowl and squeeze in the juice from the lemon.

2 Add the yoghurt and sugar and beat everything until smooth.

3 Transfer to an ice-cream maker and freeze according to the manufacturer's instructions.

4 If you don't have an ice-cream maker, pour the mixture into a freezerproof container and pop it in the freezer until almost frozen.

5 Remove the container from the freezer and beat well with a whisk to remove any ice crystals. Return the container to the freezer.

6 Repeat once more, then freeze until solid.

7 Transfer to the fridge about 20 minutes before serving.

8 Meanwhile, to make the wafers, turn the oven on to 180°C (350°F) Gas 4.

9 Put the butter and sugar into a bowl and beat with a wooden spoon until smooth.

10 Add the egg whites and beat until well mixed. Add the flour and beat until smooth.

11 Place little spoonfuls of the mixture onto the baking trays and swirl around with the back of a spoon to make thin rounds about 3–4 cm across.

12 **Ask an adult to help you** put the trays in the oven and bake for about 8–10 minutes, until golden.

13 **Ask an adult to help you** remove the trays from the oven and leave to cool.

14 Meanwhile, break the chocolate up into pieces and pop it in a small heatproof bowl. **Ask an adult to help you** set the bowl over a saucepan of gently simmering water, making sure that the bottom of the bowl does not touch the water. Stir the chocolate with a wooden spoon until it has melted. Take it off the heat and leave it to cool for a while.

15 Dip a fork into the melted chocolate and pass it to and fro over the wafers to make a pretty pattern. Leave to set.

16 When you are ready to make up the mini-sandwiches, simply sandwich 2 wafers together with a scoop of the ice cream and eat straightaway!

summer

buttermilk pancakes

225 g plain flour

3 teaspoons baking powder

½ teaspoon salt

4 tablespoons caster sugar

50 g unsalted butter,
    plus extra for frying

125 ml milk

125 ml buttermilk

2 medium eggs, lightly beaten

1 teaspoon vanilla extract

maple syrup, to serve

crispy rashers of smoked
    bacon, to serve (optional)

makes 16–18

1 Set a large sieve over a large mixing bowl. Tip the flour, baking powder, salt and sugar into the sieve and sift into the bowl. Make a well in the centre.

2 **Ask an adult to help you** melt the butter in a small saucepan over low heat or in the microwave on a low setting.

3 Put the milk, buttermilk, eggs, melted butter and vanilla extract in a jug and whisk with a balloon whisk. Pour into the dry ingredients in the bowl and whisk until the batter is smooth.

4 Put a knob of butter in a large, heavy frying pan. **Ask an adult to help you** set it over medium heat. Allow the butter to melt, swirling it so that it coats the bottom of the pan evenly.

5 Drop 4 tablespoons of the pancake batter into the hot pan and cook for about 1 minute, or until bubbles start to appear on the surface. Using a spatula, flip the pancake over and cook the other side until the pancake is golden and well risen. Remove the pancake from the pan and keep it warm on a plate covered with aluminium foil.

6 Repeat with the remaining batter.

7 Serve the pancakes with crispy bacon, if you like, and a drizzle of maple syrup.

What better way to start a sunny Sunday morning than with a mile-high stack of these pancakes? Serve with a good glug of maple syrup and rashers of crispy smoked bacon.

Did you know that the word 'tortilla' in Spanish means 'little cake'? This is the Spanish version of an omelette, but it's nice and filling because it's made with potatoes and cheese.

potato & onion tortilla

3 small potatoes, peeled

5 eggs

2 tablespoons olive oil

2 spring onions

40 g Cheddar, grated

freshly ground black pepper

a frying pan with a heatproof handle that you can put under the grill

makes enough for 4

1 Put the potatoes into a small saucepan and pour water over the top – just enough to cover them. **Ask an adult to help you** turn on the hob. Bring to the boil, then lower the heat, cover the pan with the lid and boil for 10 minutes, or until just tender. Drain and leave to cool until the potatoes are cool enough to handle.

2 In the meantime, break the eggs into a small bowl, pick out any pieces of shell, then season with a little black pepper. Beat lightly with a fork and set aside.

3 Carefully trim the hairy root ends off the spring onions, and the dark green leafy tops. Rinse the onions well under the cold tap, and drain thoroughly. Slice into thin rounds.

4 **Ask an adult to help you** heat the olive oil in a large frying pan over gentle heat, add the spring onions and cook very slowly until soft, about 4–5 minutes. Stir the spring onions occasionally with a wooden spoon.

5 When the potatoes are colder, cut each one into thick slices.

6 Turn the grill on and wait for it to heat up.

7 Add the potatoes to the frying pan and cook for a few more minutes. Stir very carefully so that you do not break up the potatoes.

8 Pour the beaten eggs into the pan and stir gently so that the egg covers the bottom of the pan. Turn the heat down to its lowest setting and cook the tortilla (without a lid on) for about 3 minutes until there is only a little runny egg left on the top.

9 Sprinkle the grated cheese all over the top and **ask an adult to help you** put the tortilla under the grill for 2 minutes, or until the egg is cooked.

10 Leave to cool slightly, then **ask an adult to help you** slide the tortilla out of the pan and onto a chopping board. Cut into squares.

Puff pastry is such a great ingredient to use. You can buy it ready-rolled, so all you have to do is unroll it, cut it into squares, rectangles or circles and top with anything you like!

easy tomato tarts

375 g ready-rolled puff pastry

4 tablespoons sun-dried
   tomato paste or olive
   tapenade

20 cherry tomatoes, each one
   sliced into 3

1 ball of mozzarella cheese
   or 4 handfuls of grated
   Parmesan

a handful of fresh basil leaves

a non-stick baking tray,
   greased

makes 6

1 Turn the oven on to 200°C (400°F) Gas 6.

2 Sprinkle a little flour over the work surface. Unroll the puff pastry and cut into 6 evenly sized squares or rectangles and transfer them to the prepared baking tray.

3 Spread a little sun-dried tomato paste or olive tapenade over the pastry but try to leave the very edges bare.

4 Arrange the sliced tomatoes over the tomato paste and try to place them in a layer rather than piling them up.

5 Tear the mozzarella cheese into little pieces and put some on top of the tomatoes.

6 **Ask an adult to help you** put the tray in the oven and roast for 15 minutes or until the pastry is golden and puffed up and the mozzarella has melted.

7 **Ask an adult to help you** take the baking tray out of the oven and sprinkle fresh basil leaves over the tarts.

Squidgy rice and firm, sweet little peas make this risotto a winner! It's super convenient as you can use either fresh or frozen peas – whatever you can most easily find.

pea & parmesan risotto

1 medium onion

2 garlic cloves

2 tablespoons virgin olive oil

300 g Italian arborio rice

120 g peas (fresh or frozen)

about 750 ml hot vegetable
    stock

20 g unsalted butter

100 g freshly grated
    Parmesan cheese

a few sprigs of fresh flat leaf
    parsley

sea salt and freshly ground
    black pepper

serves 4

1 Peel the onion and chop it into very small pieces. Peel the garlic cloves and crush them with a garlic crusher.

2 **Ask an adult to help you** put the olive oil in a medium, heavy-based pan over very low heat. Stir in the onion and garlic and cook gently for about 10 minutes so the onion turns clear and not brown. Stir in the rice (don't wash it first), then stir in the peas.

3 Turn up the heat to medium and add a ladle of the hot vegetable stock. Stir gently so it doesn't splash you, and as soon as the liquid is absorbed by the rice, add another ladle of stock.

4 Keep on stirring the rice very gently the whole time so it doesn't stick to the bottom or sides of the pan, and keep on adding the hot stock. It will take about 20 minutes of stirring

before the rice is tender. Taste a few grains with a teaspoon, but let it cool first so you don't burn your mouth. The mixture should be creamy and moist, but not dry or very wet and soupy – the exact amount of stock you will need depends on the brand of rice you use and how fast the rice is cooking.

5 As soon as the rice is tender, turn off the heat. Stir in the butter, a little salt and pepper, plus half the grated cheese.

6 Cover the pan with the lid and leave to rest for 4–5 minutes.

7 Snip the parsley into small pieces with kitchen scissors. Uncover the pan, sprinkle the parsley on top, then serve immediately with the extra grated cheese.

If you have some chicken left over from a Sunday roast, why not make this Chinese-inspired salad? There are peanuts in the dressing, so check first that no one is allergic to nuts.

bang bang chicken

400 g ready-cooked boneless chicken, such as smoked chicken, cold roast chicken or cold turkey

1 medium cucumber

1 large carrot

salad leaves, such as crispy lettuce or Chinese leaves, about 75 g

for the bang bang dressing

5 tablespoons crunchy peanut butter

1 spring onion

1 teaspoon sesame oil

1 teaspoon soy sauce

1 teaspoon caster sugar

1 teaspoon Chinese white rice vinegar or cider vinegar

1 teaspoon rice wine or water

3 tablespoons hot water

serves 4

1 Remove any skin from the chicken and discard. Pull or cut the chicken into shreds the size of your little finger, then put onto a plate.

2 Rinse the cucumber. Cut off the ends and discard. Cut the cucumber in half lengthways, then in half crossways. Cut each piece into lengthways slices the width of your little finger. Put on another plate.

3 Peel the carrot with a vegetable peeler, then cut off the ends and discard.

4 Make carrot ribbons by 'peeling' the carrot with the peeler to make ultra-thin, long strips.

5 Rinse the salad leaves and dry thoroughly in a salad spinner or pat dry with kitchen paper. Tear any large leaves into bite-sized pieces. Arrange the leaves on a serving dish. Scatter the cucumber sticks and carrot ribbons over the leaves. Lastly, arrange the chicken on the top.

6 To make the dressing, put the peanut butter in a small bowl. Carefully trim the hairy root ends off the spring onion, and the dark green leafy tops. Rinse the onion well under the cold tap, and drain thoroughly. Slice into thin rounds and add to the peanut butter.

7 Add the sesame oil, soy sauce, sugar, vinegar, rice wine or water and hot water to the bowl. Stir gently until well mixed. Taste the dressing – it should be a harmonious balance of salty, sweet and sour flavours, so add more vinegar, sugar or soy as you think is needed.

8 The dressing should be just thin enough to spoon over the chicken, so if it is too thick, stir in another tablespoon or so of hot water.

9 When the sauce seems perfect, spoon it over the chicken and serve.

rosemary focaccia

6 tablespoons olive oil

a large handful of fresh
   rosemary, leaves only

500 g strong white bread
   flour

1 x 7-g sachet easy-blend
   (fast-action) dried yeast

1 teaspoon salt

about 200 ml lukewarm
   water

rock salt

a baking tray, about 20 x
   30 cm, dusted with flour

makes 1 loaf

1 Put the olive oil and rosemary into a bowl. Squeeze the rosemary with your hands to infuse the oil.

2 Put the flour, yeast and salt into a bowl and stir well. Stir in 2 tablespoons of the rosemary-infused olive oil and 1–2 tablespoons warm water. Put your hands right in the bowl and mix the ingredients with your fingers. Keep adding warm water, a little at a time, until you get a soft but not sticky dough.

3 Sprinkle a little flour over the work surface. Flour your hands, then gently knead the dough for 5–10 minutes. It should be very smooth and pliable.

4 Using a rolling pin, roll the dough out into a rectangle slightly smaller than the prepared baking tray. Lift it carefully into the tray, cover the tray with a clean tea towel and leave it to rise in a warm place for about 1 hour, until the dough is double the original size.

5 Turn the oven on to 200°C (400°F) Gas 6.

6 Uncover the dough, which should be almost bursting out of the tray by now! Push your thumb all over it (don't worry if this deflates it) to make big dimples. Pour the remaining rosemary-infused oil all over the bread and scatter some rock salt over the top.

7 **Ask an adult to help you** put the bread in the oven and bake for 20–25 minutes. **Ask an adult to help you** remove it from the oven and tip it upside down onto a wire rack, then tap the underside with your knuckles. The bread is cooked if it sounds hollow. If it sounds like a dull 'thud', bake it for 5 minutes more.

8 Leave to cool on the wire rack until cool enough to cut into squares.

This is a dense
Italian bread with
the lovely flavour of
fresh rosemary.

If you like the focaccia on page 56, you'll love these. They're like bread rolls, so they make great picnic or lunchbox food. Eat them with butter or filled like a sandwich.

mini-focaccias with courgettes

400 g strong white bread
    flour
1 x 7-g sachet easy-blend
    (fast-action) dried yeast
3 tablespoons olive oil
about 200 ml lukewarm
    water
2 small courgettes
sea salt
2 large baking trays,
    dusted with flour

makes 8

1 Put the flour, yeast and 1 teaspoon salt into a bowl and stir well. Stir in just 2 tablespoons of the olive oil and 1–2 tablespoons warm water. Put your hands right in the bowl and mix the ingredients with your fingers. Keep adding warm water, a little at a time, until you get a soft but not sticky dough.

2 Sprinkle a little flour over the work surface. Flour your hands, then gently knead the dough for 5–10 minutes. It should be very smooth and pliable.

3 Divide the dough into 8 pieces and knead each piece again until smooth. Using a rolling pin, roll each piece into small circles just over 1 cm thick. Lay the circles, spaced well apart, on the prepared baking trays and leave to rise in a warm place for about 40 minutes, until double their original size.

4 Turn the oven on to 220°C (425°F) Gas 7.

5 Chop the ends off the courgettes and throw away. Take one courgette at a time and grate it carefully into a bowl with a cheese grater. Season with a little salt. Add the remaining oil and toss well with your hands.

6 Scatter the grated courgettes over the mini-focaccias.

7 **Ask an adult to help you** put the bread in the oven and bake for about 10–15 minutes. **Ask an adult to help you** remove one from the oven and tap the underside with your knuckles. The bread is cooked if it sounds hollow. If it sounds like a dull 'thud', bake it for 5 minutes more.

8 Serve warm, or leave to cool on a wire rack.

You know summer is in full swing when fresh broad beans appear in the supermarket (or in your garden). They are delicious mixed with bacon and grated cheese and stirred into pasta.

pasta with broad beans & bacon

1 garlic clove, peeled

200 g good-quality chopped
  bacon – look out for lardons
  or pancetta cubes (this is
  slightly smoked and tastes
  delicious)

170 ml double cream

400 g dried pasta of your
  choice (this sauce works
  really well with spaghetti
  or linguine)

350 g shelled broad beans

fresh basil leaves or mint
  (optional)

sea salt and freshly ground
  black pepper

grated Parmesan, to serve

makes enough for 4

1 Using a rolling pin, slightly squash the garlic clove. This will help to release the garlicky flavour into the sauce.

2 **Ask an adult to help you** put a frying pan on the hob over high heat. Add the bacon bits and fry for 1 minute. Turn the heat down, add the clove of garlic and fry, stirring with a wooden spoon, until the bacon is cooked and just beginning to go slightly crisp.

3 Add the double cream and stir. Turn off the heat and leave to one side.

4 **Ask an adult to help you** cook the pasta. Bring a big saucepan of water to the boil and add a pinch of salt. Drop in the pasta and cook according to the instructions on the packet.

5 Four minutes before the pasta has finished cooking, add the broad beans to the pasta pan and cook.

6 **Ask an adult to help you** drain the pasta and beans and tip them back into the empty pasta pan.

7 Taste the sauce and add the fresh herbs, if you are using them. Season with black pepper.

8 Add the sauce to the pan with the cooked pasta and broad beans. **Ask an adult to help you** heat it up gently over low heat until warmed through, mixing occasionally.

9 Sprinkle the cheese over the top and serve.

If you are vegetarian, or you are cooking for vegetarian friends or family, this is a really useful pasta recipe to learn. Everyone seems to love it, even non-vegetarians. You don't need many ingredients, and there's a good chance you already have things like sultanas and pine nuts in your kitchen storecupboard. This recipe will also make you realise that pasta doesn't need to be covered in sauce or cheese to be yummy!

pasta butterflies with courgettes, sultanas & pine nuts

2 tablespoons sultanas
3 medium courgettes
2 garlic cloves
3 tablespoons olive oil
3 tablespoons pine nuts
1 unwaxed or organic lemon, washed
400 g dried farfalle pasta
sea salt and freshly ground black pepper

serves 4

1 Put the sultanas into a little dish and cover them with hot water. Leave them for about 15 minutes, until they are nice and plump.

2 Chop the ends off the courgettes and throw away. Cut the courgettes into thin slices.

3 Peel the garlic cloves and crush them with a garlic crusher.

4 **Ask an adult to help you** heat the olive oil in a large saucepan, then fry the courgettes over medium heat for 6–8 minutes, until they are golden; you will need to give them a good stir now and again.

5 Add the pine nuts and cook for a further 2–3 minutes, until they are golden.

6 Add the garlic and cook for just 2 minutes; you don't want it to cook so much that it browns, which is when it becomes bitter.

7 Carefully grate the lemon zest.

8 Drain the sultanas and stir them into the mixture together with the lemon zest. Season the mixture with some salt and black pepper.

9 In the meantime, **ask an adult to help you** cook the pasta. Bring a big saucepan of water to the boil and add a pinch of salt. Drop in the pasta and cook according to the instructions on the packet. The cooked pasta should be 'al dente'.

10 Drain the pasta and toss with the courgette mixture.

This is the simplest of pasta dishes; but the simplest food can often be the most magical. If you like chillies, follow this recipe, but add a couple of chopped chillies or a pinch of chilli flakes with the garlic-infused olive oil. Never be afraid to experiment – that's how we discover new things!

spaghetti with herbs & garlic

400 g dried spaghetti

a pinch of salt

1 unwaxed or organic lemon, washed

a large handful of mixed fresh herbs, e.g. chives, parsley and basil, leaves torn

100 ml olive oil

3 garlic cloves, peeled (see Tip, right)

freshly grated Parmesan, to serve

serves 4

1 **Ask an adult to help you** cook the pasta. Bring a big saucepan of water to the boil and add a pinch of salt. Drop in the pasta and cook according to the instructions on the packet. The cooked pasta should be 'al dente'.

2 Grate the lemon zest and set aside.

3 While the spaghetti is cooking, **ask an adult to help you** heat the oil in a frying pan over medium heat.

4 Add the whole garlic cloves to the frying pan and leave to warm and infuse the oil for 3–4 minutes.

5 **Ask an adult to help you** fish the garlic out of the oil with a slotted spoon.

6 Drain the pasta and toss with the infused oil, the lemon zest and the herbs. Serve at once with freshly grated Parmesan.

TIP It can be fiddly to peel a garlic clove as the skin tends to stick to the garlic. Here's an easy trick: put the clove flat on a chopping board. Take a wide, blunt knife and place it, flat-side down, on top of the clove and push down hard with your hand. This loosens the skin and makes peeling much quicker!

green rice

1 green pepper

2 spring onions

a big handful of mixed fresh herbs, e.g. flat leaf parsley, chives, coriander

2 garlic cloves, peeled

3 tablespoons olive oil

225 g basmati rice

600 ml chicken stock

makes enough for 4

1 Cut the pepper in half and scoop out the seeds with your fingers. Cut the pepper halves into big pieces and **ask an adult to help you** put them into a food processor.

2 Carefully trim the hairy root ends off the spring onions, and the dark green leafy tops. Rinse the onions well under the cold tap, and drain thoroughly. Chop into pieces, then put them in the food processor.

3 Using scissors, snip off the ends of the herb stalks and put the herbs into a food processor. Add the peeled garlic cloves, too.

4 Put the lid on the food processor and **ask an adult to help you** run the machine until you get quite a smooth green paste.

5 **Ask an adult to help you** heat the olive oil in a heavy-based saucepan.

6 Remove the lid from the food processor and spoon the paste into the saucepan. Cook gently, stirring every now and then with a wooden spoon, for about 5 minutes.

7 Add the rice and fry for a few more minutes – keep stirring to make sure that you coat the rice in the green paste.

8 Add the stock, bring to a simmer and then cover the pan with the lid. Cook gently for 14 minutes.

9 **Ask an adult to help you** take the pan off the hob, then leave the rice (with the lid still on) for another 10 minutes to finish cooking.

This is a great accompaniment to chicken or fish.
Always ask an adult to help you with a food processor
and remember that the blade in the middle of the
processor is very sharp.

To make this sweet focaccia – perfect for a special breakfast – choose summer plums which are sweet but not too squidgy, or they will ooze and make the bread soggy.

sweet plum focaccia

450 g Italian type '00' flour

1 x 7-g sachet easy-blend (fast-action) dried yeast

a pinch of salt

80 g caster sugar

60 g unsalted butter

about 200 ml lukewarm water

for the topping

3-4 ripe but firm plums

1 tablespoon caster sugar

a rectangular baking tray, 20 x 30 cm, dusted with flour

makes 1 loaf

1 Put the flour, yeast, salt and sugar into a bowl and stir well.

2 **Ask an adult to help you** melt the butter in a small saucepan.

3 Stir the melted butter into the bowl with the flour mixture. Pour in 1–2 tablespoons warm water. Put your hands right in the bowl and mix the ingredients with your fingers. Keep adding warm water, a little at a time, until you get a soft but not sticky dough.

4 Sprinkle a little flour over the work surface. Flour your hands, then gently knead the dough for 5–10 minutes. It should be very smooth and pliable.

5 Using a rolling pin, roll the dough out into a rectangle slightly smaller than the prepared baking tray. Lift it carefully into the tray, cover the tray with a clean tea towel and leave it to rise in a warm place for about 1 hour, until the dough is double the original size.

6 Turn the oven on to 200°C (400°F) Gas 6.

7 Slice the plums in half and remove the stones. Cut the plums into thin slices and dab them on some kitchen paper to remove any extra juice. Push them gently but firmly into the top of the focaccia – either in neat lines or randomly, but in a single even layer.

8 Scatter over the sugar and **ask an adult to help you** transfer the tray to the oven. Bake the bread for about 25 minutes. **Ask an adult to help you** remove it from the oven and tip it upside down onto a wire rack, then tap the underside with your knuckles. The bread is cooked if it sounds hollow. If it sounds like a dull 'thud', bake it for 5 minutes more.

9 Serve warm or at room temperature.

baked alaska

1 Turn the oven on to 180°C (350°F) Gas 4. Put the greased cake tin on a sheet of greaseproof paper and draw around it. Using scissors, cut inside the line so you have a circle the same size as the tin. Fit this into the bottom of the tin.

2 Sift the flour and baking powder into a mixing bowl. Stir in the sugar. Add the very soft butter and vanilla extract to the bowl.

3 Break the eggs into a small bowl. Pick out any pieces of shell, then lightly beat the eggs and the milk with a fork to break them up. Pour the eggs into the mixing bowl. Beat all the ingredients with a wooden spoon, or **ask an adult to help you** use an electric mixer or whisk, until the mixture is very smooth and light. Spoon the cake mixture into the prepared tin and spread it around evenly.

4 **Ask an adult to help you** put the sponge cake in the oven and bake for 25 minutes, or until a light golden brown. To test if the cake is cooked, **ask an adult to help you** remove it from the oven and gently press it in the

middle. If it springs back it is cooked; if there is a dimple, then bake for 5 minutes more.

5 **Ask an adult to help you** remove the sponge from the oven, leave for 2 minutes, then run a round-bladed knife around the inside of the tin and carefully turn out the cake onto a wire rack and leave to cool completely. Turn off the oven.

6 Remove the ice cream from the freezer and leave until soft enough to spoon onto the sponge. Put the sponge cake onto a baking tray, then scoop or spoon the ice cream on top to make an even layer. Put the whole thing back into the freezer and leave until very firm – at least 1 hour, but you can leave it in the freezer for up to 3 days.

7 When you are ready to finish the Alaska, turn the oven on to 220°C (425°F) Gas 7.

8 Put the egg whites into a very clean mixing bowl. Stand the bowl on a damp cloth to keep it from wobbling. **Ask an adult to help you** use an electric mixer or whisk to whisk the egg

Imagine how proud you'll be when you bake this and serve it up for dessert after a special meal! If you want to serve it with something, make a sauce with ripe strawberries mashed using a fork or a blender and mixed with a little bit of icing sugar.

whites until they turn into a stiff white foam. Lift out the whisk and there will be a little peak of white standing on the end.

9 Quickly whisk the caster sugar into the egg whites to make a stiff, glossy meringue.

10 Remove the sponge and ice cream from the freezer. Arrange the raspberries on top of the ice cream. Quickly cover the whole thing with the meringue, spreading it evenly. Make sure that there are no holes or gaps and the meringue covers every single millimetre of the cake and ice cream. Sprinkle with sifted icing sugar.

11 **Ask an adult to help you** put the Alaska in the oven and bake for just 4–5 minutes, until lightly browned.

Like the Easy Tomato Tarts on page 50, these summer tartlets make great use of shop-bought, ready-rolled puff pastry. And they're so pretty!

white chocolate & raspberry tartlets

300 g ready-rolled puff pastry
100 g white chocolate
2 eggs
100 ml double cream
50 g caster sugar
300 g raspberries
icing sugar, to dust
a 12-hole muffin tin
a cookie cutter roughly
   the same size as the muffin
   tin holes

makes 12

1 Turn the oven on to 180°C (350°F) Gas 4.

2 Sprinkle a little flour over the work surface. Unroll the puff pastry and cut the dough into rounds using the cookie cutter. Gently press each round into a muffin tin hole.

3 Break the chocolate up into pieces and pop it in a small heatproof bowl. **Ask an adult to help you** set the bowl over a saucepan of gently simmering water, making sure that the bottom of the bowl does not touch the water. Stir the chocolate with a wooden spoon until it has melted. Take it off the heat and leave it to cool for a while.

4 Break the eggs into a large bowl, pick out any pieces of shell, then beat until smooth.

5 Whisk the cream and sugar into the bowl.

6 Whisk in the melted chocolate and make sure the mixture is nice and smooth.

7 Carefully fill the tartlet cases with the mixture using a small spoon.

8 **Ask an adult to help you** put the muffin tin in the oven and bake for about 15 minutes, or until the pastry is puffy and golden and the filling has risen (don't worry, it will fall as the tarts cool).

9 **Ask an adult to help you** remove the tin from the oven and leave to cool.

10 Put 3 or 4 raspberries on the top of each tartlet, dust with icing sugar and serve.

triple choc cookies

125 g unsalted butter,
  softened

100 g caster sugar

100 g light muscovado sugar

1 large egg

225 g plain flour

2½ tablespoons cocoa powder

½ teaspoon baking powder

½ teaspoon bicarbonate
  of soda

a pinch of salt

100 g dark chocolate chips

100 g white chocolate chips

2–3 non-stick baking trays
  (ungreased)

Makes 24 cookies

1 Turn the oven on to 180°C (350°F) Gas 4.

2 Put the butter and caster and muscovado sugars into the bowl of an electric mixer (in which case you will need **an adult to help**) or a mixing bowl. Beat with the whisk attachment or a wooden spoon until the mixture looks very soft and fluffy. Scrape down the sides of the bowl with a plastic scraper every now and then so all the ingredients get fully beaten up.

3 Break the egg into a small bowl, remove any pieces of shell, then add to the bowl and beat well until smooth.

4 Set a large sieve over the mixing bowl. Tip the flour, cocoa powder, baking powder, bicarbonate of soda and salt into the sieve, then sift these ingredients into the bowl. Mix in with the wooden spoon, or with the electric mixer on low speed.

5 Add all the chocolate chips to the bowl and mix in with a wooden spoon until everything is thoroughly combined.

6 To make the mixture into cookies, dip your hands in cold water so they are just damp then take a small amount of the mixture – about a rounded tablespoon – and roll it into a ball. Set the ball onto the prepared baking tray, then make 23 more balls in the same way. Set the balls about 3 cm apart on the trays.

7 **Ask an adult to help you** put the cookies in the oven and bake for 15 minutes.

8 **Ask an adult to help you** carefully remove the trays from the oven and leave to cool for 5 minutes before transferring the cookies to a wire rack. Leave to cool completely, then store in an airtight container. Eat your cookies within a week of baking them.

Everyone's got to have a favourite chocolate chip cookie recipe, and this is the one for you if you're a real fan of chocolate! If you want a less sweet cookie, replace the white chocolate chips with walnut pieces.

mini strawberry cakes

175 g unsalted butter,
  softened

175 g golden caster sugar

a few drops of vanilla extract

3 eggs

175 g self-raising flour

2 tablespoons milk

for the icing

2 ripe, juicy fresh
  strawberries

175 g icing sugar

a handful of strawberries,
  to decorate

a 12-hole cupcake tin, lined
  with 12 paper cupcake
  cases

makes about 12

1 Turn the oven on to 180°C (350°F) Gas 4.

2 Put the soft butter, sugar and vanilla extract in a large bowl and beat with a wooden spoon until the butter is soft, creamy and pale.

3 Break the eggs into a small bowl and remove any pieces of shell.

4 Add a little egg to the creamed butter mixture and beat with the wooden spoon. Add a little more egg and beat again. Keep doing this until you have added all the eggs.

5 You can add a little flour if the mixture looks as though it is starting to separate.

6 Set a large sieve over the mixing bowl. Tip the flour into the sieve, then sift it into the bowl. Fold it gently into the mixture with a big spoon. Don't beat or over-stir the mixture – gentle folding introduces air into the mixture and will make the cakes lovely and light.

7 Add a little milk – just enough so that the mixture softens enough to drop easily from the spoon – this is called 'dropping consistency'.

8 Spoon the mixture into the paper cases until each one is about is two-thirds full. **Ask an adult to help you** put the cakes in the oven and bake for 13–15 minutes until risen and golden and the cakes are springy to touch. **Ask an adult to help you** take the tin out of the oven and leave to cool a little. Put the cakes on a wire rack to cool down while you make the icing.

9 To make the icing, mash the strawberries in a big bowl with a fork, add the icing sugar and mix until quite smooth. Spoon the icing onto the cakes and top with chopped or whole strawberries. You may need to add a little liquid depending on how juicy the strawberries are. You can either add another strawberry, which will make the icing a stronger pink colour, or you can just add a few drops of water.

This is a lovely recipe to make with a friend on a summer's day. You'll have lots of fun decorating the little cakes, and you should top them with the sweetest, juiciest strawberries you can find.

Vegetables in cakes? It might sound horrible but in fact, adding grated courgettes to the mixture keeps the cake moist, without making it taste of courgette. Try it and see if you like it!

chocolate & courgette cake

3 courgettes (about 450 g),
   peeled
250 g unsalted butter,
   softened
250 g light brown soft sugar
2 teaspoons vanilla extract
3 eggs
125 ml milk
350 g self-raising flour
1 teaspoon baking powder
4 tablespoons cocoa powder
greaseproof paper
a cake tin, 30 x 20 cm,
   greased

makes about 20 squares

1 Turn the oven on to 180°C (350°F) Gas 4. Cut a piece of greaseproof paper the width of your cake tin and a little bit longer. Lay the paper in the tin so it goes up the sides.

2 Grate the courgettes using the smaller holes on the grater and set aside.

3 Put the soft butter, sugar and vanilla extract in a large bowl and beat with a wooden spoon until the butter is soft, creamy and pale.

4 Break the eggs into a small bowl and remove any pieces of shell.

5 Add a little egg to the creamed butter mixture and beat with the wooden spoon. Add a little more egg and beat again. Keep doing this until you have added all the eggs. Add the milk and whisk together.

6 Set a large sieve over the mixing bowl. Tip the flour, baking powder and cocoa powder into the sieve, then sift it into the bowl. Fold it gently into the mixture with a big spoon.

7 Stir in the grated courgettes and mix well.

8 Spoon the cake batter into your tin. **Ask an adult to help you** put the tin in the oven and bake for 35–45 minutes. To test if the cake is cooked, **ask an adult to help you** remove it from the oven, then push a cocktail stick into the centre. If the stick comes out clean, then the cake is ready. If it is sticky with mixture, then cook the cake for another 5 minutes.

9 **Ask an adult to help you** take the tin out of the oven. Leave to cool, then tip the cake out onto a wire rack and cut into squares.

What a beautiful tart to make for a party! A slice of this is like a little bit of summer sunshine on your plate. Glazing the pastry case with melted chocolate adds an extra special touch, but it also means you can fill the case with the fruit ahead of time without the pastry going soggy.

summer fruit tart

80 g dark chocolate

for the pastry

175 g unsalted butter, softened

75 g caster sugar

1 egg yolk

250 g plain flour

for the filling

250 g mascarpone cheese

2 tablespoons caster sugar

1 kg mixed summer berries, e.g. strawberries, raspberries and blueberries

a 23-cm loose-bottomed tart tin, greased

a pastry brush

serves 6

1 To make the pastry, put the butter and sugar into a bowl and beat with a wooden spoon until smooth.

2 Add the egg yolk and beat again until it is well mixed in. Stir in the flour and mix until you get a soft but not sticky dough.

3 Divide the dough in half. Put half into a plastic bag and freeze it to use next time.

4 Sprinkle a little flour over the work surface, turn the dough out onto it and roll out with a rolling pin until it is just a little bit bigger than the tart tin.

5 Sprinkle a little flour over the rolling pin to stop it being sticky. Roll the pastry over the rolling pin, lift it all up and carefully unroll it over the tart tin.

6 Press the pastry gently into the corners and repair any holes with a little extra pastry.

7 Trim the edges so that the pastry case is nice and neat, then pop it into the fridge for 30 minutes or so, to firm up.

8 Turn the oven on to 180°C (350°F) Gas 4.

9 Take the tart tin out of the fridge and transfer to the oven. Bake for 10–15 minutes, until crisp and golden. Remove from the oven and leave to cool.

10 Break the chocolate up into pieces and pop it in a small heatproof bowl. **Ask an adult to help you** set the bowl over a saucepan of gently simmering water, making sure that the bottom of the bowl does not touch the water. Stir the chocolate with a wooden spoon until it has melted. Take it off the heat and leave it to cool for a while.

11 Using a pastry brush, paint the base of the pastry with the melted chocolate and leave it to set.

12 To make the filling, put the mascarpone and sugar in a bowl and beat until smooth. Spoon it into the tart case.

13 Scatter the berries evenly over the mascarpone and serve in slices.

autumn

carrot soup

1 kg carrots
1 onion
1 garlic clove (unpeeled)
olive oil, for drizzling
a 400-ml tin of coconut milk
400 ml vegetable stock
a small handful of fresh
   herbs, e.g. parsley and
   coriander
a heavy-based roasting tin

makes enough for 4

1 Turn the oven on to 180°C (350°F) Gas 4.

2 Peel the carrots. Chop the ends off and throw away. Cut the carrots into chunks.

3 Peel the onion and cut it into wedges.

4 Put the onion and carrots into the roasting tin, add the garlic and drizzle with a little oil. **Ask an adult to help you** put the tin in the oven and roast for 30 minutes.

5 Halfway through the cooking time, **ask an adult to help you** take the tin out of the oven and using a spatula or big spoon, carefully turn the vegetables over so that they cook evenly all over.

6 At the end of the cooking time, **ask an adult to help you** take the tin out of the oven and carefully spoon the vegetables into a food processor. Squeeze the roasted garlic clove out of its skin and into the processor.

7 Add half the coconut milk, put the lid on and **ask an adult to help you** run the machine until you have a smooth soup.

8 **Ask an adult to help you** pour the puréed soup into a saucepan. Add the rest of the coconut milk and the stock.

9 Using kitchen scissors, snip the fresh herbs straight into the saucepan.

10 Heat the soup gently over medium heat. Taste the soup – you might like to add more stock if you want it to be thinner in texture.

A bowl of hot soup is what you really want when it starts getting chillier outside. This tastes really sweet and creamy but it's so easy because you hardly need any ingredients to make it delicious.

Unlike the Pea & Parmesan Risotto on page 53, this one is like a cheat's version because you pop it in the oven and forget about it, so you don't have to stand at the hob and stir!

oven risotto with tomatoes, peas & tuna

4 spring onions

2 garlic cloves

2 tablespoons olive oil

200 g Italian arborio rice

a 400-g tin of chopped
tomatoes with herbs

400 ml hot vegetable stock

2 x 185-g tins of tuna in oil or
spring water, drained

100 g peas (fresh or frozen)

3 tablespoons freshly grated
Parmesan

a few fresh basil leaves,
to garnish

sea salt and freshly ground
black pepper

a medium-sized heavy
flameproof, ovenproof
casserole with lid

serves 4–5

1 Turn the oven on to 180°C (350°F) Gas 4.

2 Carefully trim the hairy root ends off the spring onions, and the dark green leafy tops. Rinse the onions well under the cold tap, and drain thoroughly. Slice into thin rounds.

3 Peel the garlic cloves and crush them with a garlic crusher.

4 Spoon the olive oil into the casserole. Set the casserole on the hob and **ask an adult to help you** gently heat it. Using a wooden spoon, stir in the spring onions and garlic and cook very gently for 1 minute.

5 Tip the rice into the casserole and stir well. Cook gently for 1 minute then stir in the contents of the tin of tomatoes, followed by the stock and tuna. Stir well, then add the peas and a little salt and black pepper. Stir once more then cover the casserole with the lid.

6 **Ask an adult to help you** put the casserole in the oven and bake for 35 minutes.

7 **Ask an adult to help you** remove the casserole from the oven.

8 Before serving, remove the lid, then scatter over the grated Parmesan and the torn basil.

sticky maple ribs with roast sweetcorn

for the sticky maple ribs

1 medium red onion

3 tablespoons maple syrup

3 tablespoons soy sauce

3 tablespoons tomato ketchup

1½ tablespoons mild mustard

1½ tablespoons
Worcestershire sauce

1.2 kg spareribs

freshly ground black pepper

a large, non-stick roasting tin

for the roast sweetcorn

4 fresh corn-on-the-cobs

75 g unsalted butter

an ovenproof dish, large
enough to take the
sweetcorn in a single
layer, oiled

serves 4

1 Turn the oven on to 190°C (375°F) Gas 5.

2 Peel the skin away from the onion and throw it away. Carefully grate the onion into a large mixing bowl using the coarse or large hole side of a grater.

3 Add the maple syrup, soy sauce, tomato ketchup, mustard, Worcestershire sauce and 4 grinds of black pepper. Mix together well.

4 Add the ribs to the bowl one at a time and use a metal spoon to thoroughly cover the ribs with the sticky glaze. Carefully lift the ribs into the roasting tin. Wash your hands thoroughly before doing anything else.

5 **Ask an adult to help you** put the roasting tin in the oven and bake for 30 minutes.

6 **Ask an adult to help you** remove the tin from the oven. Using kitchen tongs, carefully turn over the ribs so they brown evenly.

7 **Ask an adult to help you** put the tin back in the oven and bake for another 30 minutes.

8 The ribs should be a dark golden brown and crispy around the edges. **Ask an adult to help you** lift the tin out of the oven and serve.

Roast sweetcorn

1 Turn the oven on to 190°C (375°F) Gas 5.

2 If the corn still has its green leafy covering it must be 'shucked' – pull off the leaves from the top pointy end, then pull off all the silky hairs.

3 **Ask an adult to help you** melt the butter: either put it in a small saucepan over the lowest possible heat, or microwave it in a bowl on medium for about 20 seconds.

4 Pour the butter into the prepared ovenproof dish, add a little black pepper, then put the corn into the dish and turn them so they are well coated in butter.

5 **Ask an adult to help you** put the dish in the preheated oven and bake for 30 minutes. **Ask an adult to help you** turn the corn over twice during this time, using kitchen tongs. Leave to cool slightly before eating.

For this recipe you need good meaty spareribs or king ribs. To complete the meal, roast some corn-on-the-cobs in the oven at the same time as you cook the ribs, so that everything is hot and ready to eat at the same time.

This is possibly the most important – and simplest – Italian recipe you'll ever need. Master this and there will be a world of scrumptious meals at your fingertips!

basic egg pasta

300 g Italian type '00' flour
a pinch of salt
3 eggs
a pasta machine (optional)

serves 4

1 Sift the flour and salt into a large bowl. Make a well in the centre and add the eggs. If you like, you can use a food processor instead – just **ask an adult to help you** put the flour, salt and eggs in the bowl of the food processor ready for mixing.

2 Bring the mixture together by mixing the ingredients with your fingertips, or press the 'pulse' button on the food processor repeatedly to make the ingredients combine. You should have a soft but not sticky dough.

3 Sprinkle a little flour over the work surface, then turn out the dough onto it. Flour your hands and gently knead the dough, stretching it and kneading it (see Tip, opposite), for about 5 minutes. Wrap the dough in clingfilm and put it in the fridge for at least 30 minutes.

4 If you have a pasta machine, set the lasagne rollers to the widest setting. Take a quarter of the pasta dough out of the fridge and keep the remaining dough wrapped in clingfilm.

5 Flatten your small lump of dough until it fits through the rollers of the machine. **Ask an adult to help you** flatten the dough by passing it through the machine.

6 Take the flattened dough and fold it into 3. Run it through the machine again and then fold it into 3 once more. Repeat this process another 3 times, so that the dough has gone through the machine on the same setting a total of five times. The dough should be nice and smooth and pliable.

7 Reduce the roller width by one notch and pass the pasta through again.

8 Repeat the process, reducing the roller width by one notch each time. You may have to cut the pasta sheet in half to fit into the machine. If you do, remember to keep the dough you are not working with covered with clingfilm because it will become too dry to work with if it is left exposed to the air for too long.

9 Once the dough has been through the smallest roller width, you can then make spaghetti (very narrow strands), tagliatelle (narrow strands) or pappardelle (wide strands) by passing your sheet of pasta through the right settings of your machine (follow the instructions in the manual), or you can **ask an adult to help you** cut the pasta with a knife. Alternatively, you can use the sheets to make lasagne, ravioli (*page 92*) or belly-button pasta parcels (*page 94*).

10 If you don't have a pasta machine, you will need to sprinkle a little flour on the work surface and roll out the dough with a rolling pin. It will take some effort and strength to get the dough super-thin, but keep at it! It may be easier for you to roll out a quarter of the dough at a time (remember to keep the remaining dough wrapped in clingfilm so that it doesn't dry out).

TIP To knead dough, push the heels of your hands into the lump of dough and squash down. Swivel the dough around slightly and squash down again. Keep swivelling and turning the dough over so that you are kneading it evenly all over. If it gets too flat, fold the dough over onto itself to make it into a lump again and keep kneading. You'll end up with a firm, smooth, stretchy dough!

tuna ravioli

1 recipe Basic Egg Pasta
   (*page 90, Steps 1–3 only*)
a pinch of salt

for the filling
2 slices of white bread
2 x 240-g tins of tuna in olive
   oil, drained
50 g Parmesan, freshly
   grated
4 tablespoons ricotta cheese

to serve
50 g unsalted butter
a small handful of fresh
   chives
1 small unwaxed or organic
   lemon, washed (optional)
a pastry wheel (optional)
greaseproof paper, dusted
   with semolina

serves 4

1 To make the filling, **ask an adult to help you** cut the crusts off the bread and whiz the bread in a food processor until you get crumbs.

2 Put the breadcrumbs, tuna, Parmesan and ricotta together in a large bowl and mix with a fork until well combined and quite smooth. Set aside.

3 Take your Basic Egg Pasta dough and follow Steps 4–8 on page 90.

4 Cut the piece of pasta into 2 rectangles roughly the same shape and size.

5 Sprinkle a little flour over the work surface and lay the 2 pieces of pasta out onto it. Cover one piece with clingfilm.

6 Place teaspoonfuls of the tuna filling at even intervals in a row across one half of the pasta. Fold the edge nearest you over to meet the edge that is furthest away and let it fall loosely over the filling. Press firmly around the filling to seal the pasta, then cut into squares using a sharp knife or pastry wheel. Lay the ravioli out on the prepared greaseproof paper.

7 Repeat with the rest of the pasta dough.

8 **Ask an adult to help you** cook the ravioli. Bring a big saucepan of water to the boil and add the salt. Drop in the ravioli and cook for 2–3 minutes until the parcels rise to the surface and are cooked but still firm.

9 In the meantime, **ask an adult to help you** melt the butter in a large frying pan over medium heat. Using kitchen scissors, snip the chives straight into the pan.

10 Drain the pasta and toss it into the chive butter, stirring gently. Cook for 2–3 minutes, until the pasta is well coated in the butter and is nice and hot.

11 If you'd like some lemon zest in your pasta too, carefully grate the zest and sprinkle over your ravioli.

Now that you know how to make pasta, you can experiment with shapes and fillings. These big floppy parcels of tuna and cheese make a lovely supper.

belly-button pasta parcels
stuffed with pumpkin

1 recipe Basic Egg Pasta
   (*page 90, Steps 1–3 only*)
50 g unsalted butter
8 fresh sage leaves
sea salt and freshly ground
   black pepper

for the filling
250 g pumpkin or butternut
   squash
leaves from 3–4 sprigs
   of fresh thyme
2 tablespoons olive oil
4 tablespoons ricotta cheese
50 g Parmesan, freshly
   grated, plus extra to serve
a pastry wheel (optional)
greaseproof paper, dusted
   with semolina

serves 4

1 Turn the oven on to 200°C (400°F) Gas 6.

2 **Ask an adult to help you** peel the pumpkin or squash, remove the seeds and cut the flesh into small chunks. Put in a roasting tin and scatter over the thyme.

3 Drizzle with olive oil, season with salt and black pepper and toss well using your hands. **Ask an adult to help you** put the roasting tin in the oven and roast for 25 minutes, or until soft and golden.

4 **Ask an adult to help you** remove the roasting tin from the oven, then leave to cool. When cool, transfer to a bowl and mash with a fork until smooth. You can use a food processor or stick blender if you prefer.

5 Stir in the ricotta and Parmesan, have a little taste and if you think it needs a touch more salt or pepper, then add some.

6 Take your Basic Egg Pasta dough and follow Steps 4–8 on page 90.

7 Cut the piece of pasta into 2 rectangles roughly the same shape and size.

8 Sprinkle a little flour over the work surface and lay the 2 pieces of pasta out onto it. Cover one piece with clingfilm.

9 Place teaspoonfuls of the filling at even intervals in a row across one half of the pasta. Leave a space of about 3 cm between each little pile.

10 Fold the edge nearest to you over to meet the edge that is furthest away and let it fall loosely over all the little mountains of filling. Using a finger, push the pasta dough gently but firmly around the pasta dough, to seal in the filling. Make sure you have no big bubbles of air. It might take a little practice, but it's fun and very satisfying when you can do it!

11 Use a pastry wheel or sharp knife to cut semi-circles, leaving a ½-cm border around the filling. Press around the edges again to make sure the packages are tightly sealed.

12 Take hold of one of the filled shapes at each corner, pull them together until they meet and pinch them together tightly. You should end up with a plump belly button.

Now that it's autumn, you'll be seeing lots of pumpkins and colourful squashes in the shops and markets. They make a tasty filling for these cute pasta parcels.

13 Repeat with all the filled parcels, then lay them on the prepared greaseproof paper.

14 Repeat the whole process with the rest of the pasta.

15 Ask an adult to help you cook the pasta parcels. Bring a big saucepan of water to the boil and add the salt. Drop in the parcels and cook for 2–3 minutes until they rise to the surface and are cooked but still firm.

16 In the meantime, **ask an adult to help you** melt the butter in a large frying pan over medium heat. Add the sage so that the butter becomes infused while it melts. Drain the pasta and toss it into the butter, stirring gently. Cook for 2–3 minutes, until the pasta is well coated in the butter and is nice and hot. Serve at once, with extra Parmesan.

If you're getting tired of eating the same old sandwiches at school every day, why not try these savoury scones, filled with cream cheese, celery and chives? They're also nice with a bowl of soup, like the Carrot Soup on page 84, or the Butternut Squash Soup on page 141 (without the croutons).

little savoury scones

50 g unsalted butter
250 g self-raising flour
a pinch of salt
50 g Parmesan, freshly grated
150 ml milk
1 small egg

for the filling
1 celery stick
3–4 fresh chives
100 g cream cheese
a pastry cutter (optional)
a baking tray
a pastry brush

makes 8

more fillings to try
100 g soft cheese and 2 slices
    of Parma ham, chopped
100 g hard cheese, grated,
    and 1 chopped tomato
2 boiled eggs, mashed and
    mixed with 1 teaspoon
    snipped fresh chives
a small tin of tuna in olive oil,
    drained and mixed with
    ½ small chopped onion and
    1 small chopped tomato

1 Turn the oven on to 200°C (400°F) Gas 6.

2 Chop the butter into cubes and put in a large mixing bowl. Set a large sieve over the mixing bowl. Tip the flour and salt into the sieve, then sift these into the bowl.

3 Put your hands in the bowl and rub the butter and flour together between your fingers and thumbs until the mixture looks like very small, fine breadcrumbs.

4 Stir in the Parmesan.

5 Start pouring in the milk, a little at a time. Keep mixing everything with your hands and adding milk until you have a soft but not sticky dough.

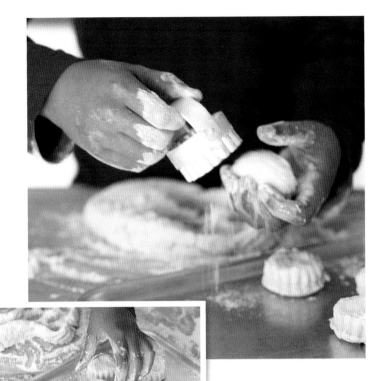

6 Sprinkle a little flour over the work surface and turn the dough out onto it. Using a rolling pin, roll it gently into a circle about 2 cm thick.

7 Cut the dough into rounds using a pastry cutter or a small, upside-down glass and lay the circles on the baking tray, leaving a little space between each.

8 Break the egg into a small bowl, remove any pieces of shell, then add 1 tablespoon water and beat lightly with a fork until it's well mixed. This is an egg wash.

9 Using the pastry brush, paint the tops of the scones with the egg wash. This will make the scones glossy when they're baked.

10 **Ask an adult to help you** transfer the tray to the oven and bake for 8–10 minutes, until the scones are firm and golden. Remove them and leave them to cool on a wire rack.

11 In the meantime, trim the ends of the celery and pull off some of the nasty stringy bits from the outside. Chop the celery finely. Using kitchen scissors, snip the chives. Put the cream cheese in a bowl and mix in the celery and snipped chives.

12 Carefully cut the scones in half and spread some of the cheesy filling on each cut side.

Just as tortillas are Spanish omelettes, so frittatas are the Italian equivalent. They're often cooked on the cooker and finished off under the grill, but this one is easier because it's simply baked in the oven. It's made with pieces of Italian bacon (pancetta lardons) and leeks, but you could try other vegetables – courgettes, onions, mushrooms, peas, tomatoes, beans – plus your favourite cheese too.

leek frittata

3 leeks

100 g pancetta lardons

2 tablespoons olive oil

8 large eggs

a small handful of fresh chives

sea salt and freshly ground black pepper

a round ovenproof dish with a diameter of about 23 cm

serves 4

1 Turn the oven on to 200°C (400°F) Gas 6.

2 Cut off the bottom of the leeks and cut off any thick, dark leaves at the top. Cut the leeks in half along their length and wash them very well – sometimes grit can get caught between the leaves.

3 Cut the leeks into fine slices and scatter them over the base of the ovenproof dish.

4 Scatter over the pancetta lardons and drizzle with the olive oil.

5 **Ask an adult to help you** pop the dish in the oven and roast for about 15 minutes, or until the pancetta is cooked and the leeks are softened.

6 In the meantime, break the eggs into a bowl, remove any pieces of shell, then beat until smooth. Season with salt and black pepper.

7 **Ask an adult to help you** remove the hot dish from the oven and put it on a heatproof surface. Carefully pour in the eggs, taking care not to touch the hot dish.

8 Using kitchen scissors, snip the chives into pieces and scatter over the frittata.

9 **Ask an adult to help you** return the dish to the oven and bake for about 20 minutes longer, until the eggs are set.

10 **Ask an adult to help you** take the dish out of the oven. Serve it warm or cold.

'Toad-in-the-hole' is a funny name for little sausages cooked in Yorkshire pudding batter. Choose your favourite sausages – pork, beef, lamb, chicken or vegetarian. Eat them with baked beans or gravy, and some steamed green vegetables on the side. Don't worry if they don't look very pretty – they'll still taste great!

toad-in-the-hole

115 g plain flour

a pinch of salt

a pinch of freshly ground
   black pepper

2 large eggs

250 ml milk

a small handful of fresh
   chives

4 tablespoons vegetable oil

12 tiny chipolata sausages
   or cocktail sausages, or
   6 larger sausages cut in half

a large tray or roasting tin

a 12-hole muffin tin

makes 12 individual toads

1 **Ask an adult to help you** adjust the oven shelves – you will be using the middle one for the muffin tin, so make sure there is plenty of room for the batter to rise above the tin. Put a shelf under the middle one and put a large tray or roasting tin on it to catch any drips. Turn the oven on to 220°C (425°F) Gas 7.

2 To make the batter, put the flour, salt and pepper in a large bowl. Make a well in the centre, then carefully break the eggs into the well (removing any pieces of shell). Pour the milk into the well, too.

3 Using a balloon whisk, mix the eggs with the milk. Start to mix the flour into the hollow. When all the flour has been mixed in, whisk the batter well to get rid of any lumps.

4 Using kitchen scissors, snip the chives into 3-cm-long pieces and whisk them into the batter. (The batter can be made up to 3 hours before you start cooking.)

5 Put 1 teaspoon of oil into each hole of the muffin tin, then **ask an adult to help you** put it into the oven to heat. **Ask an adult to help you** remove the tin after 5 minutes – the oil will be very hot – and put it on a heatproof work surface. Carefully put 1 chipolata or half a large sausage in each hole, then **ask an adult to help you** put the tin back in the oven for 5 minutes.

6 Pour or ladle the batter into a large jug and stir it once or twice.

7 **Ask an adult to help you** remove the hot tin as before, then stand back (the oil can splutter) and carefully pour the batter into each hole so each one is half full. Gently replace the tin in the oven and bake for about 20 minutes, or until golden brown and crispy.

8 **Ask an adult to help you** remove the tin from the oven and ease each toad out of its hole with a round-bladed knife.

To 'stir-fry' means exactly that – you stir the food in the pan while you fry it. The key to a good stir-fry is to chop all the vegetables first and get all the ingredients ready – once you start 'stir-frying' it is all very quick!

courgette stir-fry

2 courgettes

1 onion

1 garlic clove

a small piece of root ginger

2 teaspoons sesame oil

2 teaspoons vegetable oil

2 large handfuls of green
  beans

a little reduced-salt soy sauce

a large handful of fresh herbs
  e.g. parsley or mint,
  if you like

freshly cooked, hot egg
  noodles or rice, to serve

makes enough for 4

1 Cut off the ends of the courgettes and discard. Cut the courgettes in half lengthways, then in half crossways. Cut each piece into lengthways slices the width of your little finger. Put on another plate. You want the pieces of courgette to roughly match the shape of the greens beans so that everything cooks at the same speed.

2 Peel the onion and chop it into fairly small pieces. Peel the garlic clove and crush it with a garlic crusher. Carefully grate the ginger using the smaller holes on the grater.

3 **Ask an adult to help you** heat the sesame and vegetable oils in a heavy-based frying pan or wok, then add the onion and fry for a few minutes until it looks soft and pale gold.

4 Add the ginger, garlic, courgettes and green beans to the pan and fry for another few

minutes. Keep stirring and mixing everything so that it cooks evenly.

5 Add the soy sauce and continue to stir-fry, tossing everything together.

6 If you'd like to add some herbs, using kitchen scissors, snip the herbs into small pieces and scatter over the top.

7 Add the cooked noodles or rice to the pan and stir through until nicely mixed.

8 You can use almost any vegetables you like in a stir-fry, as long as you cut them the same size. Try some carrots, red onions or spring onions. You can also add beansprouts for extra crunch. Experiment with different seasonings like Chinese five-spice or if you like a bit of heat, add a little fresh or dried chilli.

chicken poached in milk & lemons

2 small, unwaxed or organic
   lemons
a 2.5-kg chicken
30 ml olive oil
1 whole garlic bulb, cloves
   separated but left unpeeled
a small handful of fresh sage
1 litre whole milk
sea salt and freshly ground
   black pepper

serves 6

1 Cut each lemon into 6 wedges.

2 Season the chicken by sprinkling salt and black pepper evenly all over it.

3 **Ask an adult to help you** heat half the olive oil in a large saucepan and cook the chicken, breast-side down, for 4–5 minutes, until golden. Turn the chicken over and cook for 3–4 minutes more.

4 **Ask an adult to help you** remove the chicken from the pan and pour away any used oil.

5 Pour the remaining olive oil into the pan and add the lemon wedges and garlic. Stir-fry for 2–3 minutes, until golden. Add the sage and cook for another minute or so.

6 Return the chicken to the pan and pour the milk over it.

7 Put a lid on the pan, leaving a little opening to allow for the steam to escape. Simmer over gentle heat for about 1 hour, until the meat is cooked through and the sauce has curdled into sticky nuggets (take care to keep the heat low, or the milk will reduce too quickly to fully cook the chicken).

8 **Ask an adult to help you** remove the pan from the heat. Leave the chicken to rest for 4–5 minutes before slicing.

Poaching is a no-fuss kind of cooking. Here, the chicken ends up fabulously juicy, and the milk and lemons bubble down to make sticky, citrussy nuggets. The best thing is that you hardly have to do any work, because you can leave the chicken to cook on the hob for an hour while you put your feet up!

This is a really quick dessert or afternoon treat to make, because you just mix everything together and wait for it to set. It doesn't even need to be baked.

chocolate salami

200 g milk or dark
   chocolate
50 g unsalted butter
150 g Petit Beurre or Rich
   Tea biscuits

makes 8–10 slices

1 Break the chocolate up into pieces and put it in a small heatproof bowl with the butter. **Ask an adult to help you** set the bowl over a saucepan of gently simmering water, making sure that the bottom of the bowl does not touch the water. Stir the chocolate with a wooden spoon until it has melted. Take it off the heat and leave it to cool for a while.

2 Break the biscuits into small pieces and tip them into a bowl.

3 Pour the melted chocolate mixture into the crumbled biscuits, making sure to scrape all the chocolate from the sides. Stir well.

4 Put your hands right in the bowl and bring the mixture together into a big lump.

5 Lay a large piece of clingfilm on the work surface in front of you and put the chocolate lump onto it. Form it roughly into a long salami shape.

6 Roll the clingfilm around it tightly, and as you are doing so, try to pull it into a firm, neat salami shape.

7 Twirl the ends of the clingfilm together, then pop it into the fridge to set for an hour or so. Serve in slices.

Making these pretty biscuits is the perfect way to while away a rainy afternoon. Fill some with jam and some with chocolate spread.

little filled flower biscuits

90 g unsalted butter, softened

60 g icing sugar

1 egg yolk

150 g Italian type '00' flour

jam or chocolate spread,
   to fill

icing sugar, to dust

2 baking trays

2 cookie cutters, 5 cm and
   1 cm

makes about 10

1 Turn the oven on to 180°C (350°F) Gas 4. Line the baking trays with greaseproof paper.

2 Put the butter and sugar into a mixing bowl and beat with a wooden spoon until smooth.

3 Add the egg yolk and beat again until it is well mixed in.

4 Stir in the flour and mix until you get a soft but not sticky dough.

5 Sprinkle a little flour over the work surface, turn the dough out onto it and roll out with a rolling pin until it is about 2 mm thick. Using the larger cookie cutter, stamp out rounds from the dough.

6 Take the smaller cookie cutter or a small upside-down glass and cut out a small hole in the centre of half the large rounds. Remove the centre pieces; the biscuits with the holes will make the tops. Gather up the leftover trimmings and reroll them to make more circles until all the pastry is used up.

7 Lay the circles on the prepared baking trays.

8 **Ask an adult to help you** transfer the trays to the oven and bake the biscuits for about 6–8 minutes, until crisp and light golden. **Ask an adult to help you** remove the trays from the oven and leave to cool.

9 When the biscuits are cold, spread a little jam or chocolate spread over one of the complete rounds and place one of the biscuits with the holes on top. Repeat with the remaining biscuits, then dust with a little icing sugar. Store in an airtight tin until ready to serve.

There's nothing like a warm fruit crumble on a cold evening. Use any mixed berries you can find in the freezer aisle of the supermarket.

juicy fruit crisp

2 large Granny Smith apples, or 2 peaches, or 2 medium pears

250 g fresh or frozen raspberries, blueberries or blackberries

2 tablespoons caster or demerara sugar

crisp crumble topping

125 g plain flour

80 g demerara sugar

90 g unsalted butter

a medium ovenproof baking dish, greased

serves 4

1 Turn the oven on to 190°C (375°F) Gas 5.

2 Peel the apples or pears (there is no need to peel peaches) with a vegetable peeler. Cut out the core with an apple corer or by cutting the fruit into quarters, then cutting out the core with a small knife. Cut the peaches in half, then twist to separate the halves. The stone may come out easily, but if not, cut the peach away from the stone. Discard the skin and cores, then cut the apples, pears or peaches into chunks the size of half your thumb.

3 Put the fruit in the dish, then add the berries. Sprinkle with the sugar and toss gently until just mixed. Spread the fruit evenly in the dish.

4 To make the crisp crumble topping, put the flour and sugar in a mixing bowl. Chop the butter into cubes and add to the bowl. Using your hands, squeeze the mixture together until it becomes all soft and sticky and there are pea-sized lumps of dough.

5 Scatter the mixture over the fruit in the baking dish – don't press it down.

6 **Ask an adult to help you** put the dish in the oven and bake for 25 minutes, or until bubbling and golden on top.

7 **Ask an adult to help you** remove the dish carefully from the oven. Eat the crisp hot, warm or cold.

This teatime loaf is full of the tangy taste of lemons. Buy organic or unwaxed lemons if you can and wash them before using.

lemon drizzle loaf cake

175 g unsalted butter, very soft

250 g caster sugar

2 unwaxed or organic lemons, washed

3 large eggs, at room temperature

250 g self-raising flour

½ teaspoon baking powder

115 ml milk, at room temperature

100 g caster sugar, to make the drizzle topping

a 900-g loaf tin, greased greaseproof paper or non-stick baking parchment

makes 1 large cake

1 Turn the oven on to 180°C (350°F) Gas 4.

2 Cut a long strip of greaseproof paper or non-stick baking parchment the width of the greased loaf tin. Press the paper into the tin so it covers the base and the 2 short sides. Trim off any excess paper. Cut some more paper and do the same for the long sides.

3 Put the soft butter and sugar in a large mixing bowl. Grate the lemon zest straight into the mixing bowl, then set the lemons aside.

4 Break the eggs into the bowl and remove any pieces of shell.

5 Set a sieve over the bowl, put the flour and baking powder in it, then sift into the bowl. Add the milk, then beat with a wooden spoon for a couple of minutes until smooth and well mixed, with no streaks of flour.

6 Spoon the mixture into the prepared tin and spread the surface to make it smooth.

7 **Ask an adult to help you** put the tin into the oven and bake for 50–55 minutes. To test if the cake is cooked, **ask an adult to help you** remove it from the oven, then push a cocktail stick into the centre. If the stick comes out clean, then the cake is ready. If it is sticky with mixture, then cook the cake for another 5 minutes.

8 While the cake is baking, make the topping. Cut the reserved lemons in half and squeeze out the juice with a lemon squeezer straight into a small bowl. Add the sugar and stir for a minute to make a syrupy glaze.

9 When the cake is cooked, **ask an adult to help you** remove it from the oven and stand the tin on a wire rack. Prick the top of the cake all over with a cocktail stick to make lots of small holes in it. Spoon the lemon syrup all over the top so it trickles into the holes.

10 Leave until completely cold before carefully removing the cake from the tin. Peel off the lining paper. Cut the cake into thick slices. Store your cake in an airtight container and eat it within 4 days.

Cherry berry buns are packed with a mixture of dried fruit – cherries, cranberries, strawberries and blueberries. You'll find bags of these mixed dried 'berries and cherries' in supermarkets and wholefood shops, or you can also use jumbo raisins and sultanas. Why not make up your own combination? The buns are perfect as an after-school snack.

cherry berry buns

250 g plain flour

4 teaspoons baking powder

¼ teaspoon ground mixed
   spice

100 g unsalted butter,
   softened

50 g light muscovado sugar

125 g cherry berry mix
   (*see above*)

1 large egg

4–5 tablespoons milk

caster or demerara sugar,
   for sprinkling

2 non-stick baking trays,
   lightly greased

makes 18 small buns

1 Turn the oven on to 200°C (400°F) Gas 6.

2 Set a large sieve over a mixing bowl. Tip the flour into the sieve. Add the baking powder and mixed spice to the sieve and sift these ingredients into the bowl.

3 Chop the butter into cubes and add to the bowl. Work the butter into the flour by rubbing it in with the tips of your fingers. After a few minutes of doing this, the mixture will look like fine breadcrumbs.

4 Stir in the muscovado sugar and cherry berry mix and make a well in the centre.

5 Break the egg into the small bowl and remove any pieces of shell, then add just 4 tablespoons of the milk and beat the mixture with a fork just to break up the egg and mix it with the milk.

6 Pour into the well in the flour mixture. Mix all the ingredients together with a round-bladed knife to make a firm dough. If there are dry crumbs or the dough won't mix together add another tablespoon of milk.

7 Drop spoonfuls of the mixture on to the prepared trays, using about a heaped tablespoon of mixture for each bun, spacing them slightly apart. Sprinkle each bun with a little caster sugar.

8 **Ask an adult to help you** put the buns in the oven and bake for 15 minutes, or until golden brown. **Ask an adult to help you** remove the trays from the oven and leave to cool for 2 minutes. Transfer the buns to a wire rack to cool completely. Store the cherry berry buns in an airtight container and eat them within 3 days.

maple pie

1 First make the pastry, unless you are using the ready-made pastry. Put the flour and salt into the bowl of a food processor. Chop the butter into cubes and add to the bowl. **Ask an adult to help you** run the machine until the mixture looks like fine crumbs. Pour in the cold water through the feed tube and run the machine until the crumbs come together to make a firm dough. **Ask an adult to help you** remove the dough from the bowl.

2 Scatter a little flour over the work surface. Put the dough or ready-made pastry on the floured surface and gently roll out with a rolling pin to a circle about 36 cm across. Roll the circle around the rolling pin and lift it over the pie dish. Gently unroll the dough so it drapes over the tin. Carefully press the dough onto the bottom of the tin and up the sides so there are no bubbles of air. Roll the pin over the top of the flan case to cut off the overhanging dough (or snip it off with kitchen scissors). Save the pastry for the decorations. Gently use your thumbs to press the pastry sides upwards so the pastry stands about 5 mm higher than the rim of the tin. Prick the base a few times with a fork, then chill in the fridge for 20 minutes.

3 Turn the oven on to 200°C (400°F) Gas 6. Take the chilled pastry in its pie dish out of the fridge. Cut a round of non-stick baking parchment 36 cm across. Crumple the paper to make it soft then open it out and gently press it into the pastry case to cover the base and sides. Fill the case with baking beans, dried beans or uncooked rice to weigh the paper down. **Ask an adult to help you** put it in the oven and bake for 15 minutes. **Ask an adult to help you** remove the pie dish from the oven and carefully remove the paper and beans. Turn the oven down to 190°C (375°F) Gas 5 and bake the pastry case for 5 minutes more, until a light gold colour. Put a baking tray into the oven to heat up.

4 To make the filling, break the eggs into a mixing bowl or large jug. Pick out any pieces of shell. Add the maple syrup, cream and flour and mix well with a fork until smooth.

5 **Ask an adult to help you** remove the pastry case from the oven. Put the pie dish on the hot baking tray. Scatter the walnuts over the base of the pastry case. Carefully pour the filling over the nuts, then **ask an adult to help you** put it in the oven and bake for 30 minutes, or until lightly coloured.

6 Roll out the leftover pastry fairly thinly and cut into shapes using fancy cutters (maple leaves or whatever you like). **Ask an adult to help you** remove the pie from the oven and gently arrange the pastry shapes on top. Return the pie to the oven and bake for 10 minutes more.

7 **Ask an adult to help you** remove the pie from the oven and leave to cool. Eat while still warm. Sprinkle with icing sugar or maple sugar before serving.

This American pie is
a delicious tribute to
super-sweet maple
syrup, which is made
from the sap of
some maple trees.

winter

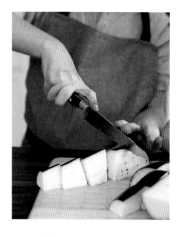

1 medium red onion
1 medium aubergine
1 red pepper
1 green pepper
2 tablespoons olive oil
2 teaspoons mild chilli powder
2 teaspoons ground cumin
2 teaspoons ground coriander
1 teaspoon dried oregano
2 x 400-g tins of chopped
   tomatoes
a 410-g tin of red kidney
   beans in water, drained
a 410-g tin of butter beans
   in water, drained
sea salt and freshly ground
   black pepper

to serve
a few sprigs of fresh coriander
a small tub of soured cream
cooked rice or flour tortillas
a large flameproof, ovenproof
   casserole with lid

serves 4–6

vegetable chilli

1 Turn the oven on to 180°C (350°F) Gas 4.

2 Peel the onion, cut it in half, then chop it into thin slices. Put on one side.

3 Rinse the aubergine and both peppers under the cold tap and drain. Trim the ends off the aubergine then carefully slice it in half from top to bottom. Set the halves on the cutting board cut or flat-side down. Cut each half into 5 long thin strips from top to bottom then cut these strips across every 1 cm. Set aside.

4 Cut the stalks off the peppers, then slice the peppers in half from top to bottom and pull out the cores and seeds. Cut the peppers into pieces about the same size as the aubergine.

5 Spoon the olive oil into the casserole. **Ask an adult to help you put** the casserole on

the hob and heat gently. Add the onions to the casserole and stir with a wooden spoon. Cook gently for 10 minutes until the onions are softened. Spoon the chilli powder, cumin, coriander, oregano and a little salt and black pepper into the casserole and stir well. Cook gently for 2 minutes, then stir again. Put the aubergines into the casserole and stir until they are coated in the onion and spice mix. Add the peppers and stir just to mix.

6 Pour the tinned tomatoes into the casserole, then stir well.

7 Stir the beans into the casserole. It might seem that there's a lot, but the vegetables will cook down and release their juices.

8 Cover the casserole with the lid and **ask an adult to help you** put it in the oven. Bake for

Everyone will love this vegetable version of chilli con carne – it's not just for vegetarians. It's not very hot, but if you like a bit more spicy heat, you can up the amount of chilli powder.

1 hour. **Ask an adult to help you** carefully remove the casserole from the oven, remove the lid and stir gently. Taste and add more salt and pepper (or chilli powder) if you think it needs some. Decorate with fresh coriander sprigs and serve with soured cream, plus cooked rice or warm flour tortillas.

350 g good-quality white bread flour

1 teaspoon salt

10 g fresh yeast OR ½ x 7-g sachet easy-blend (fast-action) dried yeast

210 ml lukewarm water

a 450-g loaf tin, lightly greased

makes 1 medium loaf

making bread

1 Put the flour in a large mixing bowl. Add the salt (and the easy-blend dried yeast if you are using this), and mix everything with your hand. Make a well in the centre of the flour.

2 If you are using fresh yeast, put it in a small bowl and break it into small crumbs with your fingers. Add half the water and stir well with a teaspoon.

3 Pour the yeast liquid into the well, then the rest of the water. If you are using the dried yeast pour all the water straight into the well in the flour mixture.

4 Using your hand, slowly stir the flour into the liquid in the well – the mixture will turn from a thick batter to a soft dough as more flour is drawn in. Work the mixture with your hand until all the flour has been mixed in – flours vary from brand to brand, so if there are dry crumbs in the bowl and the dough feels very dry and hard to mix, add a little more water to the bowl, 1 tablespoon at a time. If the dough is very sticky and sticks to your fingers or the sides of the bowl, add more flour 1 tablespoon at a time.

5 Sprinkle a little flour over the work surface and tip the dough out of the bowl onto it. Using both hands, knead the dough by stretching it out away from you then gathering it back into a ball again. Turn the ball around and stretch the dough out again then gather it back into a ball. Keep doing this for about 10 minutes – it's hard work but you can take a short rest every now and then. You can also knead the dough in a large food mixer with the dough hook attachment – it will take 4 minutes on very low speed, and you should **ask an adult to help you**.

6 Put the kneaded dough back into the mixing bowl – it now has to be left to rise. Yeast dough likes to be kept warm and moist, so cover the bowl with a snap-on lid, or put the bowl into a large, clean plastic bag (supermarket carriers work well) and tie it closed.

7 If you leave the bowl near a warm hob or above a radiator, it will take about 1 hour to double in size. At normal room temperature it will take 1½ to 2 hours, depending on the time of year. If it's in a cool unheated room, it will take 2 to 6 hours, or you can leave it overnight in the refrigerator.

8 When the dough has doubled in size, uncover the bowl and gently punch down the dough with your fist. Sprinkle your work surface lightly with flour, then tip the dough onto it. Shape the dough into a brick to fit your tin. Lift the dough into the tin and gently press it in.

9 Put the tin in a plastic bag again, and let the dough rise in a warm place until doubled in size – about 1 hour.

10 While the dough is rising, turn the oven on to 220°C (425°F) Gas 7.

11 Uncover the risen dough and **ask an adult to help you** put the tin in the oven. Bake it for 30 minutes, or until a good golden brown on top.

There are recipes for various different types of bread in this book, e.g. Rosemary Focaccia on page 56 and Irish Soda Bread on page 17. The recipe here gives you the method for a simple, traditional white loaf, but you can also make animals, pizzas or a plait from the same dough. If you feel inspired, add fruit and nuts or cheese to the dough.

12 Ask an adult to help you remove the tin from the oven and tip it upside down onto a wire rack, then tap the underside of the bread with your knuckles. The bread is cooked if it sounds hollow. If it sounds like a dull 'thud', bake it for 5 minutes more.

13 Ask an adult to help you remove the tin from the oven and tip the bread out onto a wire rack to cool.

14 The bread is best eaten within 5 days, or frozen for up to 1 month.

Curries are Indian stews, cooked slowly with lots of spices to make the meat and sauce extra-tasty. Serve this beef curry with Thai Fragrant Rice (page 31) and green beans.

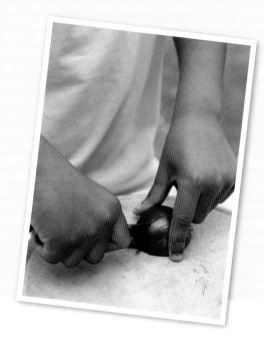

beef rendang

500 g diced braising steak

1 tablespoon tamarind purée

1 cinnamon stick

1 tablespoon dark muscovado
  sugar

2 tablespoons soy sauce

250 ml beef or vegetable
  stock

¼ teaspoon ground black
  pepper

¼ teaspoon freshly grated
  nutmeg

6 green cardamom pods

2 medium red onions

3 garlic cloves

a 3-cm piece of root ginger

serves 4

1 Put the meat in a heavy medium saucepan or casserole dish. Add the tamarind, cinnamon stick, sugar, soy sauce, stock, black pepper and nutmeg.

2 Crush the cardamom pods with a mortar and pestle (or with the end of a rolling pin). Throw away the green husks and keep the tiny black seeds. Crush the seeds and add them to the pan.

3 Peel the onions, garlic and ginger. Cut each onion in 4 and cut the ginger into thick slices. Put the onions, garlic and ginger in a food processor or blender and **ask an adult to help you** blend the mixture until it is very finely chopped, almost a coarse purée.

4 Spoon this mixture into the saucepan. Stir gently until well mixed.

5 Set the pan over medium heat and bring the mixture to the boil. **Ask an adult to help you** stir gently and carefully, then cover the pan with a lid and turn down the heat to very low so the mixture bubbles very gently.

6 Leave to cook for 1½ hours, stirring now and then. You don't have to stay and stir all the time it's cooking. In fact, you could **ask an adult** to do the stirring. Finally, remove the lid and cook uncovered for 20–30 minutes until the sauce is very thick. Remove the cinnamon stick and serve.

Potatoes roasted with rosemary and garlic are heavenly. They are the perfect accompaniment to a Sunday roast, but they also go well with sausages, lamb chops or the Meatloaf on page 137.

rosemary potatoes

1 kg floury potatoes, e.g.
  Maris Piper or King Edward
4 tablespoons olive oil
2 garlic cloves
a small handful of fresh
  rosemary leaves
sea salt and freshly ground
  black pepper

serves 4

1 Turn the oven on to 200°C (400°F) Gas 6.

2 Peel the potatoes and chop them into small chunks. Put them in a bowl, cover with water and leave them to soak for 10 minutes, then drain and pat dry with kitchen paper.

3 Pour the olive oil into a roasting tin and **ask an adult to help you** put it in the oven. Heat for 3–4 minutes until the oil is hot.

4 Peel the garlic cloves and crush them with a garlic crusher.

5 **Ask an adult to help you** to remove the tin from the oven and carefully add the potatoes, taking care that the hot oil doesn't splash. Return the tin to the oven and roast the potatoes for about 35 minutes, until crisp and golden and almost soft.

6 Using kitchen scissors, snip the fresh rosemary leaves.

7 **Ask an adult to help you** remove the tin from the oven and scatter the garlic, rosemary and some salt and black pepper over the potatoes. Stir and return to the oven for 5–10 minutes longer. Drain the potatoes on kitchen paper before serving.

Here's a pasta sauce made with minced beef – it's a little like Bolognese sauce, but even better!

tagliatelle with rich meat sauce

1 recipe tagliatelle (pages
   90-91) or 400 g shop-
   bought dried tagliatelle
sea salt and freshly ground
   black pepper
freshly grated Parmesan,
   to serve

for the sauce

1 onion
1 carrot
2 garlic cloves
1 celery stick
3 tablespoons olive oil
450 g lean minced beef
a 400-g tin cherry tomatoes
   (or regular chopped)
300 ml beef stock
1 teaspoon caster sugar
1 teaspoon mixed dried herbs

serves 4

1 Peel the onion and carrot and chop them finely. Peel the garlic cloves and crush them with a garlic crusher. Trim the ends of the celery and pull off some of the nasty stringy bits from the outside. Chop the celery finely.

2 **Ask an adult to help you** heat the oil in a saucepan and fry the onion, carrot, garlic and celery over low heat for 5–6 minutes, until everything is soft but not coloured.

3 Add the minced beef to the saucepan and break it up into pieces with a wooden spoon. Leave it to cook for 5 minutes, stirring occasionally, until it has turned brown all over.

4 Stir in the tinned tomatoes, stock, sugar and mixed herbs, then season with a little salt and black pepper. Leave the sauce to bubble for about 25 minutes, until it has reduced and is glossy and thick.

5 In the meantime, **ask an adult to help you** cook the tagliatelle. Bring a big saucepan of water to the boil and add a pinch of salt. Drop in the tagliatelle and cook for about 2 minutes if you've made it fresh, or according to the instructions on the packet if you bought it dried, from a shop. The tagliatelle is ready when it is 'al dente' (*see Tip below*).

6 Drain the pasta and toss with the sauce. Serve at once with freshly grated Parmesan.

TIP To check if pasta is perfectly cooked, **ask an adult to help you** fish out a strand of tagliatelle from the hot water, blow on it till it's cool enough to eat, then carefully take a bite. The pasta should be soft but not soggy, and should still retain a little bite to it. When it's cooked like this, it's called 'al dente'!

Pasta with pesto is one of the simplest suppers you can make. Home-made pesto is best, but you can of course buy it ready-made from the supermarket.

pasta with french beans & pesto

400 g dried pasta shapes
  of your choice
200 g French beans, snapped
  in half if they are very long
4 tablespoons Home-made
  Pesto (see below) or
  shop-bought pesto
75 g freshly grated Parmesan
freshly ground black pepper

serves 4

for the home-made pesto
½ garlic clove
a small pinch of sea salt
4 handfuls of fresh basil
  leaves
a big handful of pine nuts
2 handfuls of freshly grated
  Parmesan
about 2–3 tablespoons olive oil

*makes enough for
2 saucepans of pasta*

1 Fill a big saucepan with water, put on the hob and **ask an adult to help you** turn on the heat. Bring to the boil, then **ask an adult to help you** add the pasta and look at the pack instructions for how long to cook it.

2 Two minutes before the pasta has finished cooking, add the beans to the pan and cook.

3 **Ask an adult to help you** drain the pasta and beans and tip them back into the empty saucepan.

4 Add the pesto and carefully stir to coat the pasta with the pesto. Season with black pepper. Sprinkle the Parmesan over the top and serve.

Home-made Pesto

1 Peel the garlic and put it in a mortar with a small pinch of salt (this will help you to squash the garlic). Take the pestle and squash the garlic against the mortar.

2 Add the basil and bash the leaves.

3 Add the pine nuts and bash again. If you are using a pestle and mortar you will need to take it in turns with friends or family to help you bash everything to stop your arm from aching! It will take a good few minutes.

4 Add the Parmesan and mix together just with a spoon.

5 Spoon the mixture into a bowl and gradually add the olive oil until the sauce just drops off your spoon.

easy speedy pizzas

1 Turn the oven on to 200°C (400°F) Gas 6.

2 To make the pizza bases, set a sieve over a large mixing bowl. Tip the flour, sugar, bicarbonate of soda and salt into the sieve and sift into the bowl. Stir in the oregano.

3 Make a well in the centre of the flour and pour in the buttermilk. Using one hand, start to mix the flour into the liquid, then gradually work all the flour into the dough to make a soft and slightly sticky mixture. If there are dry crumbs and it is hard to work all the flour into the dough, add 1 tablespoon of buttermilk or milk. If the dough is really sticky and feels wet, work in more flour, a tablespoon at a time.

4 Sprinkle a little flour over the work surface. When the dough comes together in a ball, tip it out of the bowl onto the work surface. Knead the ball of dough with both hands by squashing and squeezing it for 1 minute, or until it looks smooth.

5 Divide the dough into 4 equal pieces and shape each piece into a ball. Flour your hands, then gently pat out each piece of the dough to a circle about 17 cm across. Set the circles slightly apart on the prepared baking trays.

6 Set a large sieve over a bowl, then tip the tin of tomatoes into the sieve and leave them to drain for a couple of minutes.

7 Pour the tomatoes into a food processor or blender (the juice drained off can be saved for soups or sauces). Add the tomato purée, olive oil, oregano and a pinch of salt and pepper to the processor. Peel the garlic and add it too.

8 **Ask an adult to help you** blend the tomato mixture very briefly just to make a lumpy purée. Tip the mixture into a bowl.

9 Spoon 2 tablespoons of the tomato topping onto the middle of each pizza. Spread the tomato mixture over the base, leaving a 2-cm border of uncovered dough all around the edge.

10 Slice the mozzarella or pull it into long shreds. Arrange the pieces on top of the tomato sauce on the pizzas.

11 Finally, top your choice of as many extras as you like.

12 **Ask an adult to help you** put the pizzas in the oven and bake them until they are light golden and bubbling – about 15–18 minutes.

13 **Ask an adult to help you** carefully remove the pizzas from the oven, but leave to cool for a couple of minutes before eating – the melted cheese can burn your mouth.

If you've never made pizza, you've been missing out! It's lots of fun because you can make them any size or shape you like and choose your favourite toppings.

baked polenta with cheese

1 litre well-flavoured
 vegetable stock

250 g instant polenta

100 g Parmesan, freshly
 grated

2 handfuls of baby spinach,
 torn

100 g unsalted butter,
 softened

100 g Taleggio cheese

sea salt and freshly ground
 black pepper

a baking tray, greased

a pastry cutter (optional)

a large ovenproof dish

serves 4

1 Pour the stock into a large, heavy saucepan, then **ask an adult to help you** turn on the heat. Leave the stock to heat up until it is bubbling nicely. Pour in the polenta in a steady stream, stirring quickly all the time with a large balloon whisk. Do it gently so that it doesn't splash. Cook the polenta for the time recommended on the packet you are using (some are quicker to cook than others).

2 When the polenta is cooked and thick, remove it from the heat and pop it on a heatproof work surface. Use an oven glove to hold the saucepan handle. Take a whisk and stir in the Parmesan, spinach, a little pepper and half the butter. Have a little try (making sure it's not too hot first!) and see how it tastes. Add a little salt if you think it needs it.

3 **Ask an adult to help you** pour the mixture out onto the prepared baking tray, then smooth it over with a spatula. Leave it to cool and set.

4 Turn the oven on to 200°C (400°F) Gas 6.

5 Cut the polenta into circles using a pastry cutter or an upside-down glass and lay the circles in the ovenproof dish. **Ask an adult to help you** chop the cheese into little pieces, then dot the cheese evenly over the circles of polenta. Dot the remaining butter over too.

6 **Ask an adult to help you** put the tray in the oven and bake the polenta for about 15–20 minutes, until the cheese is melted and bubbling.

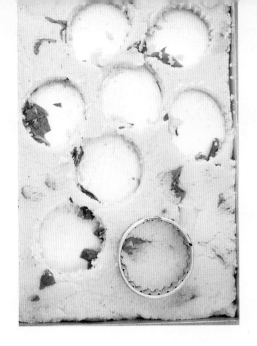

Polenta is an Italian ingredient made from dried, ground corn. When you cook instant polenta, it thickens within minutes, and is delicious with cheese and butter. This recipe makes a lovely vegetarian main course.

Try this meatloaf with the Rosemary Potatoes from page 126. You can also serve it with leftover tomato sauce.

meatloaf

1 onion
2 garlic cloves
1 egg
900 g lean minced beef
2 teaspoons dried oregano
150 g Parmesan, freshly
    grated
sea salt and freshly ground
    black pepper
a 450-g loaf tin
greaseproof paper

serves 4

1 Put the loaf tin on a sheet of greaseproof paper and draw around the base. Cut out the rectangle and lay it in the bottom of the tin to line it.

2 Turn the oven on to 180°C (350°F) Gas 4.

3 Peel and chop the onion into quite small pieces. Peel the garlic cloves and crush them with a garlic crusher. Put the onion and garlic into a large bowl.

4 Break the egg into a small bowl, remove any pieces of shell, then beat with a fork until smooth. Pour into the bowl with the onion and garlic along with the minced beef, oregano and Parmesan.

5 Season well with salt and black pepper.

6 Put your hands right in the bowl and mix the ingredients with your fingers until everything is well combined.

7 Spoon the mixture into the loaf tin and smooth the top with the back of a spoon.

8 **Ask an adult to help you** transfer the tin to the oven and cook for 45 minutes.

9 **Ask an adult to help you** remove the tin from the oven and turn the meatloaf out onto a chopping board. Cut in slices and serve.

Try to find tinned cherry tomatoes for this no-fuss oven bake, as they are tastier than regular tinned whole or chopped tomatoes. You should also buy the best-quality sausages you can afford because they will be made with good pork and have more flavour.

sausage & beans

2 red onions
12 good-quality sausages
3 tablespoons olive oil
4–5 garlic cloves
2 x 400-g tins of cherry
    tomatoes, drained and
    rinsed
250 ml good vegetable
    or meat stock
1 dried bay leaf
a 400-g tin of cannellini
    beans, drained and rinsed
a small handful of fresh
    flat leaf parsley leaves
4 slices of country-style
    bread, toasted, to serve
an ovenproof casserole dish or
    deep roasting tin

serves 4

1 Turn the oven on to 200°C (400°F) Gas 6.

2 Peel the onion, cut it in half, then chop it into thin slices. Scatter the slices over the base of the ovenproof casserole dish or deep roasting tin.

3 Scatter the sausages over the onions and drizzle everything with the olive oil.

4 **Ask an adult to help you** transfer the dish to the oven and roast for about 20 minutes, until the onions are soft and the sausages have started to colour.

5 **Ask an adult to help you** take the dish out of the oven.

6 Peel the garlic cloves and scatter them whole over the sausages in the dish.

7 Add the tinned tomatoes, stock, bay leaf and beans. **Ask an adult to help you** return the dish to the oven. Bake for 30 minutes longer, until the onions are tender and the sausages are cooked through.

8 **Ask an adult to help you** remove the dish from the oven and chop the parsley leaves. Stir in all but a spoonful of the parsley.

9 Put a slice of bread in each of 4 bowls. Spoon the sausages and beans over the bread, and some of the sauce around. Scatter the remaining parsley over the top.

This recipe makes a large pot of soup – enough to feed a hungry crowd on a cold winter's day. If you don't like things too spicy, just leave the chilli out.

butternut squash soup with cheesy croutons

1 onion

2 carrots, peeled

1 medium leek

1 celery stick

25 g unsalted butter

1 tablespoon olive oil

1 butternut squash

1 garlic clove, crushed

1 red chilli, deseeded
  and finely chopped

a 2-cm piece of root ginger,
  peeled and grated

1 litre vegetable stock

sea salt and freshly ground
  black pepper

for the croutons

6 slices of 1-day-old bread
  (preferably sourdough)

1 tablespoon olive oil

100 g Cheddar or Parmesan,
  grated

makes a large pot!

1 Peel the onion and carrots and chop them into small pieces. Cut off the bottom of the leeks and cut off any thick, dark leaves at the top. Cut the leeks in half along their length and wash them very well – sometimes grit can get caught between the leaves. Chop the leeks into small pieces. Trim the ends of the celery and pull off some of the nasty stringy bits from the outside. Chop the celery into small pieces.

2 **Ask an adult to help you** put the butter and oil in a large saucepan over medium heat. Add the chopped onion, carrots, leek and celery and cook slowly until they are soft but not browned.

3 While the vegetables are cooking, prepare the butternut squash. **Ask an adult to help you** peel the squash, remove the seeds and cut the flesh into chunks.

4 Add the squash, garlic, chilli and ginger to the pan and continue to cook for 3–4 minutes.

5 Add the stock and season with salt and black pepper. Bring to the boil, then lower the heat so that the soup is at a gentle simmer and continue to cook until the squash is tender.

6 **Ask an adult to help you** blend the soup until smooth either in a blender or using a stick blender. Check the seasoning and add more salt or pepper if needed. If the soup is a little thick, add some extra stock.

7 To make the croutons, turn the oven on to 180°C (350°F) Gas 4.

8 Cut the bread into chunks and tip into a large bowl. Add the oil and mix with your hands so that the chunks are coated in oil. Add the grated cheese and stir well. Tip the croutons out onto a baking tray. **Ask an adult to help you** put the tray in the oven and bake for 15 minutes, or until golden and crisp.

9 Ladle the soup into bowls and scatter some croutons on top.

Grissini are long, crunchy Italian breadsticks, ideal for dunking into dips or for snacking on.

cheesy grissini

375 g strong white bread
    flour

1 x 7-g sachet easy-blend
    (fast-action) dried yeast

1 teaspoon fine sea salt

200 ml lukewarm water

1 tablespoon olive oil

3 tablespoons freshly
    grated Parmesan

1–2 tablespoons sesame
    seeds (optional)

2 or more baking trays,
    lined with greaseproof
    paper

makes about 24

1 Sift the flour into a large mixing bowl and stir in the yeast and salt. Make a well in the centre and pour in three-quarters of the water and all the oil. Stir with a wooden spoon – the dough should be soft but not too sticky.

2 Add the Parmesan to the dough. It will get mixed in when you knead the dough.

3 Sprinkle a little flour over the work surface. When the dough comes together in a ball, tip it out of the bowl onto the work surface. Knead the ball of dough with both hands by squashing and squeezing it for 7 minutes, or until it looks silky smooth and elastic.

4 Shape the dough into a neat ball again. Wash and dry the mixing bowl and sit the dough back in it. Cover tightly with clingfilm and leave in a warm place until the dough has doubled in size. This can take at least 1 hour.

5 Turn the oven on to 200°C (400°F) Gas 6.

6 Tip the dough onto the floured work surface again and knead for 1 minute. Divide it into walnut-sized pieces and roll each piece into a long stick using your hands.

7 Arrange the grissini on the prepared baking trays and leave to rise again for a further 10 minutes.

8 Brush some of the grissini with water and sprinkle the sesame seeds over them, if you like. **Ask an adult to help you** put one of the baking trays on the middle shelf of the oven. Bake for 7–8 minutes, or until crisp and golden brown.

9 Now bake the remaining grissini as above, until crisp and golden brown.

Make the grissini long and bumpy and they will look like creepy witches' fingers! You can sprinkle sesame seeds on some of them before baking, if you like.

sticky toffee pudding

175 g pitted chopped dates

300 ml boiling water

1 teaspoon bicarbonate
  of soda

50 g unsalted butter,
  very soft

175 g caster sugar

½ teaspoon vanilla extract

2 large eggs, at room
  temperature

225 g plain flour

1 teaspoon baking powder

for the toffee sauce

100 g dark muscovado sugar

50 g unsalted butter

200 ml single cream

an ovenproof baking dish, about
  1.5 litre capacity, greased

makes 1 large pudding

1 Turn the oven on to 180°C (350°F) Gas 4.

2 Put the dates in a small saucepan or heatproof bowl. **Ask an adult to help you** pour over the boiling water then stir in the bicarbonate of soda and leave to soak until you're ready to use it.

3 Put the very soft butter in a mixing bowl or the bowl of an electric mixer. Add the caster sugar and the vanilla extract and beat with a wooden spoon or electric whisk (**with adult help**) until very well combined (the mixture won't look soft and fluffy like a sponge cake mix).

4 Break the eggs into a bowl, pick out any pieces of shell, then beat with a fork just to break up the eggs. Pour a little of the egg mix into the mixing bowl and beat well. Keep on adding the eggs, a little at a time, then beating well, until all the eggs have been used up.

5 Set a sieve over the bowl and tip the flour and baking powder into the sieve and sift into the bowl. Stir gently a few times to half-mix in the flour, then pour the date and water mixture into the bowl. Carefully mix the whole lot together to make a runny batter.

6 Pour the pudding batter into the prepared baking dish. **Ask an adult to help you** put the pudding in the oven and bake for about 40–45 minutes, until a good golden brown. To test if the pudding is cooked, **ask an adult to help you** remove it from the oven and push a cocktail stick into the centre; if the stick comes out clean then the pudding is cooked, if the stick is sticky with mixture then the pudding needs another 5 minutes in the oven, before you test it again.

7 While the pudding is baking, make the toffee sauce. Put the sugar, butter and cream into a small saucepan. **Ask an adult to help**

Who doesn't love sticky toffee pudding! It's so delicious, you'll want to keep coming back for more. The toffee sauce is also good with ice cream.

you set the pan over low heat and heat gently, stirring now and then until melted, smooth and hot.

8 **Ask an adult to help you** remove the pudding from the oven.

9 Serve the pudding warm with the hot toffee sauce. Any leftover pudding and sauce can be gently reheated and served again. Eat within 2 days of making.

chocolate yule log

115 g caster sugar

4 large eggs, at room
   temperature

½ teaspoon vanilla extract

40 g unsalted butter

135 g plain flour

½ teaspoon baking powder

for the filling and icing

4–5 tablespoons chocolate
   hazelnut spread (Nutella)

100 ml double cream

100 g dark chocolate

icing sugar, to sprinkle

your choice of decorations

a Swiss roll tin, 20 x 30 cm,
   greased

2 sheets of non-stick baking
   parchment

makes 1 large cake

1 Turn the oven on to 200°C (400°F) Gas 6. Cut a rectangle of non-stick baking parchment to fit the greased Swiss roll tin – set the tin on the paper, draw around it then cut just inside the line – and fit it into the tin to completely cover the base.

2 Put the sugar in a mixing bowl or the bowl of an electric mixer. Break the eggs into a small bowl, pick out any pieces of shell, then pour the eggs into the bowl with sugar. Add the vanilla extract.

3 **Ask an adult to help you** melt the butter in a small saucepan over low heat, or in the microwave. Leave to cool until needed.

4 Using an electric whisk or the whisk attachment of the mixer, **ask an adult to help you** whisk the sugar and eggs together for 2 minutes, or until very thick and foamy.

5 Set a sieve over the bowl. Tip the flour and baking powder into the sieve and sift it into the bowl. Gently fold into the egg mixture with a large metal spoon. Do this slowly and carefully so the air isn't knocked out of the mixture. Drizzle the melted butter over the top and fold it in quite quickly.

6 Pour the mixture into the prepared tin and spread it evenly using a plastic scraper or spatula. **Ask an adult to help you** put the sponge in the oven and bake for 10 minutes. To test if the sponge is cooked **ask an adult to help you** pull it out on the oven shelf and press the centre lightly with a finger; if the cake is springy it is cooked, if your finger leaves a dent, cook for 2 more minutes, then test again.

7 **Ask an adult to help you** remove the sponge from the oven. Leave for 1 minute to cool. Meanwhile cover a wire rack with a dry tea towel, then a sheet of baking parchment. **Ask an adult to help you** carefully tip the sponge out onto the paper. Peel off the lining

This is the cake the French make to celebrate Christmas. It is a sponge roll, made by whisking the eggs with an electric mixer or whisk, filled with ready-made chocolate spread, then covered with a rich chocolate cream. Dust the top very generously with icing sugar to look like beautiful snow. Complete the winter wonderland scene with decorations like robins, tiny trees, a cake candle, or a small sleigh filled with foil-wrapped sweets or coins for presents. You should be able to find all sorts of decorations like this in the run-up to Christmas in supermarkets, kitchen shops and through online suppliers of cake decorations.

paper. Gently roll up the sponge with the other sheet of paper still inside. Leave the sponge on the wire rack until it is completely cold.

8 Carefully unroll the sponge and discard the paper – don't worry if the cake has cracked, it will all be covered up, and will still taste good! Spread the chocolate spread over the sponge. Roll up the sponge and put it on a serving plate.

9 Put the cream for the icing in a small saucepan. **Ask an adult to help you** heat the cream until it is steaming hot, but not boiling. Remove the pan from the heat. Break up the dark chocolate and add it to the pan of hot

cream. Leave for 2 minutes then stir gently until smooth and melted. Leave until the mixture is thick enough to spread, about 1 hour.

10 Spread the cooled chocolate cream all over the top and sides of your cake. Run the prongs of a fork down the log so it looks like bark on a real tree. Sprinkle with sifted icing sugar, then add any decorations.

11 When you are ready to eat your cake, remove all of your decorations and cut it into slices. Your yule log is best stored in an airtight container in a cool place and eaten within 3 days (but it'll probably be eaten by then!).

christmas spice biscuits

300 g plain flour

2 teaspoons ground cinnamon

½ teaspoon ground ginger

½ teaspoon ground mixed
  spice

175 g unsalted butter, chilled

6 tablespoons clear honey

writing icing pens and silver
  balls, to decorate

a selection of shaped cookie
  cutters, such as stars,
  Christmas trees, angels,
  bells and reindeer

thin ribbon, thread or raffia,
  to hang

2 non-stick baking trays,
  greased

makes about 24

1 Put the flour, cinnamon, ginger and mixed spice in the bowl of a food processor. Chop the butter into cubes and add to the bowl of the processor.

2 **Ask an adult to help you** run the machine until the mixture looks like fine crumbs.

3 Measure the honey into the bowl of the processor and **with adult help** run the machine until the mixture comes together to make a ball of dough.

4 **Ask an adult to help you** remove the blade from the bowl, then remove the dough from the bowl. Wrap the dough in clingfilm or greaseproof paper and put it into the fridge to chill until it is firm enough to roll out – about 30 minutes.

5 Turn the oven on to 180°C (350°F) Gas 4.

6 Sprinkle the work surface and a rolling pin with flour. Gently roll out the dough until it is about 5 mm thick. Cut out shapes using your

cookie cutters. Gather up the trimmings into a ball then roll out and cut more shapes. To make Christmas decorations you can hang up you'll need to make a small hole at the top of each cookie with a cocktail stick (make sure the hole is large enough to thread your chosen ribbon through).

7 Arrange the shapes slightly apart on the prepared baking trays. **Ask an adult to help you** put them in the oven and bake for about 10 minutes, or until golden.

8 **Ask an adult to help you** carefully remove the trays from the oven and put the trays onto a heatproof surface. Leave to cool for 5 minutes. Gently transfer the cookies to a wire rack and leave until cold.

9 Decorate however you like: thread them with ribbon then ice using coloured icing pens and silver balls. Leave until set, then hang up. Eat your cookies as soon as possible or store them in an airtight container for up to 5 days.

This spiced gingerbread-like dough makes lovely Christmas biscuits. You can cut shapes out of it using festive cookie cutters and have lots of fun decorating them with coloured icing and silver balls.

These lovely chewy bars are made with a basic mixture of butter, honey, sugar, oats, flour and baking powder. You can add your own favourite dried fruits, seeds and nuts or you could replace the nuts with chopped dates, dried figs or dried cranberries. Put them in a lunchbox, save them up for an after-school snack, or enjoy them for breakfast instead of a bowl of cereal.

muesli bars

100 g unsalted butter

130 g clear honey

2 tablespoons light
   muscovado sugar

300 g porridge oats

2 tablespoons plain flour

½ teaspoon baking powder

50 g ready-to-eat dried
   apricots, chopped

2 tablespoons sunflower
   seeds

2 tablespoons sesame seeds

2 tablespoons raisins

100 g mixed nuts or dried
   fruit and nut mix, chopped

20.5 x 28 cm brownie tin,
   greased

non-stick baking parchment
   or greaseproof paper

makes 16

1 Turn the oven on to 160°C (325°F) Gas 3. Cut a rectangle from a sheet of non-stick baking parchment or greaseproof paper the same size as the greased brownie tin, and fit it into the bottom of the tin.

2 Put the butter in a large saucepan. Add the honey and sugar. **Ask an adult to help you** put the pan over low heat. Heat gently until the butter melts. Carefully remove the pan from the heat. Stir gently with a wooden spoon. Tip all the rest of the ingredients into the pan and stir well with the wooden spoon.

3 Transfer the mixture to the prepared tin and spread evenly. Press the mixture into the tin with the back of a spoon.

4 **Ask an adult to help you** put the tin in the oven and bake for 30 minutes, until golden brown.

5 **Ask an adult to help you** remove the tin from the oven and put it on a wire rack. Leave it to cool completely.

6 Loosen the mixture from the tin by running a round-bladed knife inside the edge of the tin, then flip the tin upside down onto a chopping board so the muesli mixture falls out in one piece. Cut it into 16 bars. Store your bars in an airtight container and eat them within a week.

chocolate cupcakes

175 g plain flour

1 teaspoon baking powder

a pinch of salt

25 g cocoa powder

150 g caster sugar

100 g unsalted butter,
very soft

2 large eggs

125 ml milk

for the topping

100 g dark chocolate

1 tablespoon golden syrup

25 g unsalted butter

a 12-hole muffin tin, lined
with paper muffin cases

makes about 12

1 Turn the oven on to 180°C (350°F) Gas 4.

2 Place a large sieve over a mixing bowl. Tip the flour, baking powder, salt, cocoa powder and sugar into the sieve as you measure them, then sift into the bowl.

3 Add the very soft butter to the bowl. Break the eggs into a small bowl, pick out any pieces of shell, then beat the eggs with a fork until they are a bit frothy.

4 Pour the eggs and milk into the mixing bowl. Use a wooden spoon to mix all the ingredients together to make a smooth batter.

5 Carefully spoon the cake mixture into the paper cases in the muffin tin, putting an equal amount into each one.

6 **Ask an adult to help you** put the muffin tin in the oven and bake for 20 minutes, until the cupcakes are just firm to the touch.

7 **Ask an adult to help you** remove the tin from the oven and leave to cool for about 2 minutes. Transfer the cupcakes to a wire rack and leave to cool completely.

8 While the cupcakes are cooling, make the topping. Break the chocolate up into pieces and pop it in a small heatproof bowl with the golden syrup. **Ask an adult to help you** set the bowl over a saucepan of gently simmering water, making sure that the bottom of the bowl does not touch the water. Stir the chocolate and syrup with a wooden spoon until the chocolate has melted. Take it off the heat and leave it to cool for 5 minutes.

9 To finish the cupcakes, spoon the smooth, runny chocolate topping on top of the cakes and add your decoration. Leave it to set before eating. Store your cupcakes in an airtight container for up to 4 days.

Here is something you can do on a rainy day. Bake some cupcakes and decorate them with a fudgy topping and some jelly beans or anything you like – try chocolate buttons, dolly mixtures or hundreds and thousands.

If you like carrot cake, you'll enjoy making (and eating!) these miniature versions. Get a friend or your brother or sister to help you make the cake mixture, then keep an eye on them while they bake. They don't take long!

225 g carrots

3 eggs

140 g light brown soft sugar

7 tablespoons sunflower oil

150 g plain or wholemeal self-raising flour (or half and half)

1 teaspoon mixed spice or a mixture of ground cinnamon and nutmeg

70 g desiccated coconut (if you don't like coconut add more dried fruit instead)

75 g mixed dried fruit, e.g. raisins, cranberries, blueberries

a muffin tin, lined with 12 paper muffin cases, or 12 silicone muffin cases

makes about 12

carrot muffins

1 Turn the oven on to 180°C (350°F) Gas 4.

2 Peel and grate the carrots using the smaller holes on the grater – you want the carrots to be grated finely so that they mix into the cake mixture easily.

3 Break the eggs into a large mixing bowl, pick out any pieces of shell, then beat lightly with a fork.

4 Add the sugar to the mixing bowl and whisk together with a balloon whisk or **ask an adult to help you** use an electric whisk. Whisk until thick and creamy.

5 Gradually add the oil, whisking all the time.

6 Add the flour, mixed spice (or cinnamon and nutmeg), coconut and dried fruit and stir until everything's mixed in.

7 Spoon the mixture into the paper cases in the muffin tin, putting an equal amount into each one.

8 **Ask an adult to help you** put the muffin tin in the oven and bake for 12–14 minutes, or until the muffins are cooked and golden.

9 **Ask an adult to help you** take the muffin tin out of the oven and leave to cool a little. Put the muffins on a wire rack to cool down until you are ready to eat them.

cinnamon meringues with berries

for the meringues
2 egg whites
a pinch of cream of tartar
(optional)
110 g caster sugar
¼ teaspoon ground cinnamon

for the berries
500 g frozen berries, or 125 g
each fresh blueberries and
raspberries, and 250 g
fresh strawberries
1 tablespoon icing sugar
vanilla ice cream, to serve
non-stick baking parchment
2 baking trays

serves 4-6

1 Turn the oven on to 120°C (250°F) Gas ½.

2 If you are using frozen berries, put them and the sugar in a serving bowl. Mix gently, then cover and set aside to defrost slowly – 2–4 hours.

3 Cut out 2 rectangles of non-stick baking parchment to fit the 2 baking trays, then set one on each tray.

4 Put the egg whites and cream of tartar in a large, spotlessly clean and grease-free bowl (grease will make it difficult to whisk the whites). Stand the bowl on a damp cloth to keep it from wobbling.

5 **Ask an adult to help you** use an electric whisk and whisk the egg whites. Whisk steadily until the whites turn into a stiff white foam – lift out the whisk and there will be a little peak of white standing on the end.

6 Mix the sugar with the cinnamon, then whisk it into the egg whites, 1 tablespoon at a time, to make a stiff, glossy, golden meringue.

7 Scoop 1 heaped teaspoon of the mixture out of the bowl, then use a second teaspoon to help you push the meringue onto the

prepared tray to make a craggy, mountain-like heap. Scoop out the rest of the mixture in the same way to make about 16 heaps, spaced slightly apart on the trays.

8 **Ask an adult to help you** put the baking trays into the oven and bake for 2 hours. **Ask an adult to help you** remove the trays from the oven and leave to cool. Peel the meringues off the lining paper and pile them up in a bowl.

9 If you are using fresh berries, rinse the blueberries in a colander under the cold tap. Drain thoroughly, then tip into a serving bowl. Add the raspberries, rinse the strawberries and pull out the green leafy tops. Put two-thirds of the strawberries in the bowl with the other berries. Put the rest of the strawberries in a small bowl, add the sugar and mash the berries with a fork to make a coarse, juicy purée. Tip this mixture into the bowl of berries and stir gently until just mixed. Cover and leave at room temperature until ready to serve, up to 2 hours.

10 If you are using the defrosted (frozen) berries, mash them roughly. Serve the meringues and berries with vanilla ice cream.

If you are using frozen berries here, you will need to let them defrost for a couple of hours before serving. Take them out of the freezer before you start and they should be ready by the time you finish.

index

credits & acknowledgements

The publisher would like to say a big thank you to all the lovely models who appear in this book.

The contributors

Linda Collister has three children, all of whom love good food and help out with planning, shopping and preparing meals. Linda has taught cooking in primary schools, planning hands-on lessons with the class teacher. She is a Cordon-Bleu-trained chef and the author of numerous cookbooks. For Ryland Peters & Small, she has written *Baking with Kids*, *Christmas Treats*, *Cakes & Bakes from My Mother's Kitchen*, *Brownie Bliss* and *Easy Baking*.

Liz Franklin is head chef at The Royal Oak gastropub in Wiltshire. She has three sons and has previously taught cookery classes for children. She writes for various magazines, as well as being a freelance cook and food stylist, and she recently set up a food and wine education school in Italy.

Amanda Grant is a broadcaster, food writer and mother of three young children. She has written several books including *Grow It, Cook It with Kids* and *Healthy Lunchboxes for Kids* for Ryland Peters & Small. Amanda is heavily involved in the first dedicated Children's Food Festival and travels the UK teaching children about good food and nutrition. Her television credits include GMTV's 'Back to School Campaign'.

Annie Rigg is a freelance food stylist and writer and has worked on numerous books and best-selling magazines, such as *Sainsbury's Magazine*, *Olive*, *delicious*, *Country Living* and *Good Food*. She has worked with Jean-Christophe Novelli, Ainsley Harriott, and Rachel Allen. For Ryland Peters & Small, she has also written *Christmas Cooking with Kids*, *Christmas Cupcakes*, *Birthday Cakes for Kids*, *Macarons* and *Decorating Cakes & Cookies*.

Recipe credits

Linda Collister
Baked Alaska
Bang bang chicken
Beef rendang
Cherry berry buns
Chocolate cupcakes
Chocolate fudge birthday cake
Chocolate yule log
Christmas spice biscuits
Cinnamon meringues with berries
Easy speedy pizzas
Fresh orange cake
Irish soda bread
Italian crostini
Juicy fruit crisp
Lamb koftas with pita pockets
Lemon drizzle loaf cake
Making bread
Maple pie
Mini vegetable frittatas
Muesli bars
Oatie cookies
Oven risotto with tomatoes, peas & tuna
Pea & Parmesan risotto
Salmon filo parcels
Sticky cinnamon buns
Sticky maple ribs with roast sweetcorn
Sticky toffee pudding
Thai meatballs with chicken
Toad-in-the-hole
Tomato pesto rolls
Triple choc cookies
Vegetable chilli

Liz Franklin
Baked pancake parcels with pears & mascarpone
Baked polenta with cheese
Basic egg pasta
Belly-button pasta parcels stuffed with pumpkin
Chicken poached in milk & lemons
Chocolate salami
Creamy pea soup
Leek frittata
Little filled flower biscuits
Little lemon iced yoghurt sandwiches
Little savoury scones
Meatloaf
Mini-focaccias with courgettes
Pasta butterflies with courgettes, sultanas & pine nuts
Pea, sausage & onion wraps
Penne with tomatoes, garlic & basil
Rosemary focaccia
Rosemary potatoes
Sausage & beans
Spaghetti with herbs & garlic
Summer fruit tart
Sweet plum focaccia
Tagliatelle with rich meat sauce
Tuna ravioli
White chocolate & raspberry tartlets

Amanda Grant
Carrot muffins
Carrot soup
Chocolate & courgette cake
Courgette stir-fry
Easy tomato tarts
Green rice
Green salad with croutons
Mini strawberry cakes
Pasta with broad beans & bacon
Pasta with French beans & pesto
Potato & onion tortilla

Annie Rigg
Buttermilk pancakes
Butternut squash soup with cheesy croutons
Cheesy grissini

Photography credits

Key: a=above, b=below, r=right, l=left, c=centre.

Peter Cassidy
Page 125l, 132

Vanessa Davies
Pages 20–21, 30–31, 54–55, 100–101, 110, 111r, 112l, 113, 118, 122–124, 133, 156–157

Tara Fisher
Pages 8, 9c, 10–11, 44, 45r, 48–53, 60–62, 66–67, 76–77, 78l, 79, 84–85, 102–103, 125c, 125r, 130–131, 154–155

Richard Jung
Pages 78r, 112r

Lisa Linder
Pages 5a, 5br, 6al, 6ar, 6cr, 7, 9l, 12–13, 22–25, 41–43, 45l, 46–47, 56–59, 63–65, 68–69, 72–73, 80–81, 83l, 83r, 90–99, 104–109, 119l, 127–129, 134–143, 159, 160

William Lingwood
Page 111l

William Reavell
Page 40

Polly Wreford
Pages 1–4, 5bl, 6c, 6b all, 9r, 14–19, 26–29, 32–39, 45c, 70–71, 74–75, 82, 83c, 86–89, 114–117, 119c, 119r, 120–121, 126, 144–153